Nibbling on Einstein's Brain

The Good the Bad & the Bogus in Science

By Diane Swanson

Illustrated by Warren Clark

ANNICK PRESS

TORONTO + NEW YORK + VANCOUVER

Annick Press Ltd.

We acknowledge the support of the Canada Council for the Arts, the Ontario Arts Council, and the Government of Canada through the Book Publishing Industry Development Program (BPIDP) for our publishing activities.

Edited by Jane Billinghurst
Copy-edited by Elizabeth McLean
Interior design and illustration by
   Warren Clark
Cover design by Irvin Cheung/
   icheung design
Cover illustration by Warren Clark

The art in this book was hand
   drawn and enhanced in
   Photoshop
The text was typeset in Cicero

Printed and bound in Canada

Visit us at
www.annickpress.com

Cataloguing in Publication Data

Swanson, Diane, 1944–
   Nibbling on Einstein's brain : the good, the bad and the bogus in science

Includes bibliographical references and index.
ISBN 1-55037-687-X (bound)   ISBN 1-55037-686-1 (pbk.)

   1. Science – Methodology – Juvenile literature. 2. Fraud in science – Juvenile literature. I. Clark, Warren. II. Title.
Q175.2.S92 2001   j507'2   C2001-930205-3

Distributed in Canada by: Firefly Books Ltd., 3680 Victoria Park Ave., Willowdale, ON M2H 3K1
Published in the U.S.A. by Annick Press (U.S.) Ltd.
Distributed in the U.S.A. by: Firefly Books (U.S.) Inc., P.O. Box 1338, Ellicott Station,
   Buffalo, NY 14205

To the Committee
for the Scientific Investigation
of Claims of the Paranormal (CSICOP)
in honor of its 25th anniversary

Acknowledgments

My sincerest gratitude extends to Barry Beyerstein — scientist, Simon Fraser University professor, and member of the CSICOP Executive Council — for enthusiastically reading this manuscript and suggesting several changes and additions; to Carolyn Swanson, doctoral candidate in analytical philosophy at McMaster University and the University of Guelph, for her insightful input; to John Allen Paulos of Temple University for granting permission to quote from "Who Wants to Be a Sci-Savvy President?" in his column, "Who's Counting," ABCNEWS.com, March 1, 2000; to the many scientists and other thinkers — including Stephen Barrett, Cynthia Crossen, Richard Dawkins, Martin Gardner, Robert Hazen, Cooper Holmes, Peter Huber, John Allen Paulos, James Randi, Carl Sagan, and James Trefil — whose writings both informed and inspired me; to Jane Billinghurst for her creative, thoughtful, and thorough editing; to Elizabeth, Nathan, and Taylor McLean for their helpful and supportive comments; to Warren Clark for his clever illustrations and book design; to Colleen MacMillan for her unflagging encouragement; and to Wayne Swanson for always being there.

Contents

1 Beware of Bad Science

O ne day soon, if it hasn't happened already, you'll realize you've been terribly misled. Like everyone else, you've likely made some important decisions that were based on bad science — or the bad reporting of good science. Suppose, for instance, that you bought a bottle of Dr. Smart's Cough Syrup for Grandpa without realizing that Dr. Smart did her research only on poodles, not people. What if you decided to abandon your dream of becoming a teacher because an analysis of your handwriting claimed you didn't have what it takes? Imagine you'd sworn off your favorite soft drink, Silly Soda, because a news reporter announced it can make you sick — only the reporter failed to mention you'd have to drink 40 glasses a day to feel any ill effects. ARGHHH! You've been led down the garden path — three times!

How? Well, you can't assume that whatever might clear your pet poodle's throat is going to help Grandpa. After all, there are important differences between dogs and people. And a handwriting analysis is much like a fortune cookie. It's fun to see what it has to say, but you wouldn't want to plan your life — or your career — around it. As for Silly Soda, think about it. Every day, you eat food that could be harmful if you overdid it. Take salt, for instance. Small quantities help you contract your muscles,

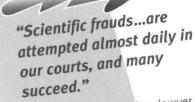

but too much might raise your blood pressure, bring on kidney stones, or trigger some heavy-duty headaches. Just because downing large amounts of something is unsafe doesn't mean that eating small amounts is necessarily bad for you.

What do you stand to lose if you don't sift out the bad science — and the bad reporting of good science — that's hidden among all the good stuff? The sky's the limit because science affects every part of your life. It influences what you eat and drink. It determines what kind of house you live in, what type of bike you ride, and how fast you can reach your friends on the Internet. It affects how you're treated when you're sick or injured, from the simple bandage you slap on a cut to the miniature video camera you may one day swallow in a pill to get the inside scoop on your ailing intestines.

Imagine what happens when inadequate, faulty, or phony science creeps into your life. It's used incorrectly to declare products "safe" or "unsafe." It persuades you to buy goods that are trash. It promotes poor medical treatments that don't help and discourages you from getting care that does. In court, it's used to back up unreliable — even false — claims. For instance, doctors have given "expert" testimony supporting people who claimed their cancer was caused by a blow from a can of orange juice or the handle of an umbrella. One doctor supported a fortune teller's testimony that a hospital CAT scan — which provides pictures of the brain — destroyed her ability to predict the future. A jury awarded her a million dollars for her loss, but a judge later threw out the decision.

"Scientific frauds...are attempted almost daily in our courts, and many succeed."

— Peter W. Huber, lawyer

Some lobby groups present bad science to sway public opinion. One famous example concerned Alar, a product that used to be sprayed on apples to keep them fresh. By the 1980s, scientists had some concern that very high doses of Alar might cause cancer in test animals. In 1989, a lobby group that was pushing to have Alar banned in the United States released the results of a single, poorly done study to the hosts of a TV news show called *60 Minutes*. Although the animals used in the study had been exposed to amounts of Alar 266 000 times greater than people would ever be, the researchers concluded Alar threatened human lives — especially the lives of small children.

Drink of Death

"Cures" that are not tested scientifically can be useless in treating illness. What's worse, they might even bring on a more serious sickness. During the 1920s, a patent medicine that claimed to cure more than 150 disorders turned out to be deadly. "Radiothor, the New Weapon of Medical Science" was laced with radium, a radioactive metal used in making luminous paints and, under controlled conditions, in treating cancer. Unlike today's drugs — which are subjected to hundreds of millions of dollars of scientific research for about 15 years before they're approved — Radiothor was never properly studied. No one knew what effects it would have on people who swallowed it daily. The man who marketed the medicine, William Bailey, had no medical or scientific qualifications. He simply insisted Radiothor was safe because he drank it himself.

One man chose to take two or three small bottles of Radiothor every day for two years to boost his energy. At first, it seemed to work, but then he lost a lot of weight. Many of his teeth fell out, and bones throughout his body started to crumble. Soon after, he died of radium poisoning. And what happened to William Bailey? When researchers dug up his remains 20 years after his death, they discovered the "medicine" had destroyed him, too. His body was still radioactive!

When *60 Minutes* featured this study, people panicked. Families and businesses pitched out their apples and apple juice, and pressed the American government to ban Alar. Even though government environmental and food agencies announced that the small amounts of Alar on apples were harmless, the public insisted Alar should go. It was withdrawn from use later that year. Whether or not it should have been will probably never be known. The point is that it was withdrawn for the wrong reason — limited, faulty research.

With all that's affected by science, it's lucky that people like you are willing to sort the good from the bad. Although it might seem like a big role to take on, you don't have to be a rocket scientist — or any other kind of scientist — to succeed. Mostly, you just have to be willing to ask questions and think clearly — something this book helps you do by setting up:

A SCIENCE WATCH (chapter 2) with "Baloney Busters" that look at how science can go wrong;

A MEDIA WATCH (chapter 3) with "Media Alerts" that look at how reporting can confuse or misrepresent science; and

A MIND WATCH (chapter 4) with "Mind Traps" that look at how the human mind — your mind — can muddle the science news you receive.

The book also suggests some winning strategies (chapter 5) that can help you, so you might as well charge right ahead and beef up your skills. Start by taking a quick peek at science.

First: The Good Stuff

Make no mistake about it: scientists conduct plenty of sound research. And where would you be without it? During the last century alone, science helped expand food supplies, wipe out several diseases, extend life expectancies, and explore space — even putting people on the Moon. Science also put you in spandex shorts and polarized sunglasses, and made it possible for you to download cool music off the Internet.

Although there are many scientific advances that make everyday living easier or more interesting, science is not just a mountain of discoveries and a mass of facts. It's a way of figuring things out and evaluating information. It's a style of thinking. So if you're going to spot bad science, first it's necessary to understand how good science operates — to become familiar with the "scientific method."

"Science is essentially a structure for asking questions and every five-year-old is a natural scientist because every five-year-old is curious about the world."

— Robert Pollack, biologist

Theoretically Speaking

Scientists develop theories — logical explanations based on scientific information — and design research to test them. They conduct experiments, making precise observations and, where possible, taking exact measurements. Just suppose Dr. Checkitout wanted to test a theory that rats swim faster after eating protein-rich peas. In her lab, she might compare the swimming speeds of a large number of rats before and after they had eaten a measured portion of peas. She might also compare these swimming speeds with those of rats before and after they had eaten a measured portion of beans. Dr. Checkitout would analyze her results and draw some conclusions. She might find, for instance, that the mean swimming speed for rats doubled after they ate peas, which seems to support her theory. But if the tests using beans produced similar results, she would have to revise her theory.

Scientists doing all types of research find that the conclusions they draw usually force them to revise or even replace their original theories. Then the new theories guide further sets of experiments and analyses, producing more conclusions that usually alter the theories again. Round and round the process goes, testing and retesting. Along the way, this scientific method helps researchers discover a lot about what something is NOT — which helps them pin down what something IS.

Faraday Wins the Day

Meet Michael Faraday (1791–1867). Not only was he a brilliant English scientist, he was considered "one of the greatest experimentalists who ever lived." And for good reason. As a young man, Faraday figured that if electricity could generate magnetism — as an electromagnet does — then magnetism could generate electricity. He based his theories not on hunches, but on the science of the times, including the experiments of William Sturgeon, who produced the first electromagnet, and Sir Humphry Davy, who discovered that copper wire attracts iron filings when electricity is passed through it. Faraday set up experiments to test his theory and failed. Tried again, and failed again. For nine years, Faraday continued to conduct experiments, analyze them, and revise his theory.

Finally, his hard work paid off. In 1831, Faraday demonstrated that he could move a wire through a magnetic field and produce electricity. Rough as it was, the world's first electric generator had been created. In fine scientific style, Faraday reported his research to his colleagues, who reviewed and tested his work. His generator became a hit worldwide, and soon, more electricity was produced Faraday-style than any other way.

Piecing It All Together

As scientists gather conclusions from their studies, a body of information grows, and scientists develop a better understanding of whatever it is they're exploring. Some of the information that emerges is tested so many times that, eventually, it becomes widely accepted. The relationship between smoking and lung cancer, for example, was established after decades of research using many different types of studies.

Sound science rarely springs from a single source. Instead, it builds on the contributions of different scientists — just as Michael Faraday built his electric generator with contributions from others in his field. Doing research is a bit like doing a gigantic puzzle where many people can watch — and join in. Each time someone completes part of the puzzle, it helps the others figure out where their pieces fit. Building on one another's solutions, scientists finish the whole puzzle faster and more easily than any one of them could by working alone.

The Human Genome Project, involving international teams of scientists and 10 years of research, is a good example. Its goal? To map all the genes — the building blocks of life — in the human body. Completed in the year 2000, this genetic map is now helping scientists all over the world discover, among other things, how genetically linked diseases might be treated — even prevented.

Cross-checking

Besides working together, scientists check one another's work. No matter how well any study is done, it's not convincing until other scientists can do it, too. Whoever repeats an experiment should be able to get results similar to those of the first scientist. If the results are not similar, the original results might be incorrect or might have come about just by chance.

"Science is an attempt, largely successful, to understand the world, to get a grip on things, to get hold of ourselves, to steer a safe course."
— Carl Sagan, astronomer

The practice of cross-checking has given rise to thousands of professional scientific journals all around the world. Their editors give reports of scientific studies to groups of scientists called "referees," who check to see that the studies meet high research standards. So strict are these standards that some of the most respected journals reject more than 80% of all the reports they receive! The referees make sure that the research methods are sound and that the results have been properly analyzed. They also find out if the experiments have been repeated by other scientists and encourage still more scientists to test the research.

This system of cross-checking and publishing is not perfect, but it helps to sort the good stuff from the bad. Scientists believe it's their right and their responsibility to test one another's research. That's how science of all kinds progresses.

Eat a Memory?

Wouldn't life be easy if you could absorb the math you need just by snacking on math-packed brains? After all, people do eat animal brains, sometimes cooked in a sauce with mushrooms and peas. And at one time, cannibals in New Guinea believed they could absorb the skills and knowledge of their enemies by eating their brains.

In the 1950s and 1960s, a group of competent scientists began experimenting with the idea of edible memories. At that time, they thought that recollections were stored in the brain as molecules of protein, so they figured that, when one animal ate another's brain, the victim's memories might be transferred to the diner.

Experiments on flatworms, rats, and goldfish seemed to support this theory. For instance, researchers trained flatworms to fear light by shocking them with electricity whenever a light was shone on them. Soon light alone was enough to make the worms cringe. Then they were chopped up and fed to flatworms that had never experienced electric shocks. But these new flatworms also cringed when light was shone on them. The research seemed to support the theory of edible memories.

However, in 1966, no fewer than 23 researchers reported to the professional journal *Science* that their own experiments did not support the findings of the edible memory studies. Thanks to the time-honored tradition of scientists cross-checking one another, the theory died. So even if you could nibble on Einstein's brain — and theoretically, you could because part of it has been preserved — it wouldn't make you any smarter.

Passing It On

The scientific knowledge that filters down over the decades is the stuff of textbooks. It's a body of facts that most scientists have come to agree on, such as Earth circles the Sun, all things are made of atoms, your heart pumps blood around your body, and — like it or not — you inherited some of your looks from your parents.

New scientific findings are just entering this long filtering process. They're mostly unproven, part of the "pioneer science" that's looking at things such as artificial intelligence — robots who are even smarter than you are — and therapies to keep you feeling young for a longer time. Still, the research in all fields of pioneer science should be consistent with the basic methods and principles of textbook science. If it's not, you shouldn't put much faith in its findings.

The Stepping Stones of Science

FACTS

THEORIES

RESEARCH

CONCLUSIONS

REVISED THEORIES

MORE RESEARCH

CROSS-CHECKS

MORE FACTS

The Faces of Science

Monkeys, stars, volcanoes, medicines, criminals. Science examines millions of different subjects. Its vast web of research contains thousands of strands, or areas of study, all following the same basic investigative routes to discovery. Most of these areas fall into one of several broad disciplines: physics, chemistry, biology, geology, and social sciences.

A physicist studies energy and matter (anything that exerts force or occupies space).

All this is NOT to say that only pioneer science is changing and developing. Even textbook science is sometimes updated. Back in the second century, Greek astronomer Ptolemy thought the Sun revolved around Earth. That fact was widely accepted for hundreds of years. Then Polish astronomer Copernicus (1473–1543) came up with quite a different theory: Earth revolved around the Sun. But it took the development of the telescope — an eye on the sky — and the work of Italian astronomer Galileo to confirm Copernicus's theory about a hundred years later, in 1632.

A chemist studies basic substances, such as hydrogen and oxygen, and how they combine to form complex substances.

A geologist studies the development of the Earth's crust.

A social scientist studies individual and group behavior and compares different cultures and economic systems.

A biologist studies living things — mostly plants and animals.

Now: The Bad Stuff

Faulty and phony research pops up in every scientific discipline and demonstrates all kinds of problems: poorly trained researchers, flawed study designs and methods, weak data, incorrect analyses, or off-base conclusions — the stuff that referees for scientific journals try to spot.

Some of this faulty science is built on hunches, not theories, and it's supported by stories, instead of scientific studies. For instance, some graphologists — people who claim to discover your character in your handwriting — think that dotting the letter *i* with a circle reveals creativity. They offer as "evidence" stories such as this: Janice and Fred both dot the letter *i* with circles, and she is an amazing pianist, while he produces marvelous oil paintings! But graphologists don't test their ideas by checking to see how many people who dot their *i*'s with circles aren't artistic, and how many people who don't dot their *i*'s that way are.

A poor researcher often develops theories that are so general they're impossible to test. For instance, Ima Fuzzhead has a "theory" that eating marshmallows causes rashes because her grandfather says that something in marshmallows affects the skin. But she hasn't thought about whether marshmallows affect some people differently than others, or whether different brands or types of marshmallows might yield different results, or whether serving size matters.

She hasn't even defined what kinds of skin rashes she is talking about. Because her theory is so vague, other scientists cannot test it to see if it's valid or not because they don't know what to test — flavored or plain marshmallows? a large serving or just a few? And they don't know exactly what they are looking for — itchy red bumps all over? raised white patches on the arms? Scientific theories are precise so that others can design experiments to test them. Science without the details is usually bad science.

Unlike good scientists, poor researchers don't welcome the criticism that could help them progress. They often don't submit their work to professional journals, where it would be questioned by scientists. Instead, they publish their findings in newspapers and popular magazines and on Internet sites, where there is no built-in mechanism for professional review and where many readers might be impressed by the research, no matter how poor it is.

Some creators of bad science know what they're doing wrong. They're deliberately out to defraud. More common are those who sincerely believe in their studies, but don't understand enough about scientific methods to recognize their mistakes. Both types fool or mislead people.

It's possible — even common — for research to look like science and sound like science without actually being science. Phony researchers may use scientific language and refer to impressive-sounding statistics without

Rumpology is the study of — you guessed it — rumps. People who practice it claim to be able to see the state of your health and love life in the lines of your rear end. Now that's hindsight!

designing scientific studies to sort facts from fancy. For instance, they might claim: "Research shows that Compound XBY12 — traced to cures used in ancient cultures — doubles the effectiveness of the body's natural healing process in 9 out of 10 cases." But they don't say what's in this compound, or who tested it and how. They don't specify which "ancient cultures" used it and with what proven results. Phony researchers don't indicate how the effectiveness of the body's "natural healing process" was measured, how many "cases" were tested in all, or how they were selected for testing.

Some of these researchers have titles that people often confuse with titles of real scientists. For instance, some alchemists try to turn lower-value metals, such as iron, into precious metals, such as gold. But don't confuse *alchemists* with *chemists,* the scientists who study the ways the Earth's elements affect one another. And don't mix up *astrologers,* who use the positions of the stars and planets to "predict" events in people's lives, with *astronomers* — scientists who study the makeup and movement of planets, stars, and other bodies in the sky.

Some of this shadow science can be worse than misleading: it can be outright harmful. Horoscopes in astrology columns, for instance, may be entertaining to read, but they're no laughing matter if they influence how you choose your date for Saturday night or — even worse — how you decide on a career. Classifying people in terms of their supposed astrological traits is no different from classifying them in terms of racial or gender stereotypes. Of course, once you recognize phony science for what it is, you can read a horoscope or your "future" in a fortune cookie just for the fun of it.

Forget It

You've likely heard of the Nobel Prizes, which recognize great scientists and others who work for the interests of humanity. But what about the Ig Nobel Prizes? Sponsored by a publication called *Annals of Improbable Research* (AIR), these comic awards recognize work that "cannot, or should not be reproduced." Their name is a play on "ignoble," meaning inferior or unimportant. The Ig Nobels highlight unusual — often goofy — research and spur an interest in science.

Starting in 1991, AIR has handed out 10 awards a year, presented by actual Nobel Prize winners. Here are a few of the science projects that have received Ig Nobels over the years.

Chonosuke Okamura of Japan won a biodiversity award for discovering what he says are fossils of more than 1000 extinct mini-species. Each of these "fossils," including dragons and princesses, is less than .03 cm (1/100 in.) long. Okamura's most famous claim is the finding of a fossilized "miniman" — about the size of an ant — who lived in a little house and knew how to make china dishes. Hmm, a case of "seeing" what you want to?

Anders Baerheim and **Hogne Sandvic** of Norway won a biology prize for studying how ale, garlic, and soured cream affected the appetite of leeches. The mind races! Ale, garlic, and soured cream — eaten individually or as one incredible mix? And as none of these foods are regular fare for leeches, what's the point of the research?

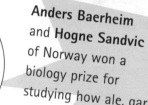

Veterinarian **Robert A. Lopez** of the United States received an entomology award for experiments with mites that infect cats' ears. He stuck some of the mites in one of his own ears to observe what they would do. Just how similar do you suppose the ear of a cat is to the ear of Dr. Lopez?

◆ ◆ ◆

The more you think about the benefits of good science and the hazards of bad, the more you'll want to be able to tell one from the other. So read on and set up your own science watch, using Baloney Busters to help you focus on some of the differences between the two. But before you do, use the checklist provided here to review the general characteristics of good science (bad science shares few or none of them). These characteristics apply to research projects big and small, including the ones you might set up for science fairs.

Good Science Checklist

✓ Science is built on theories, that is, logical explanations that are based on scientific facts.

✓ Science depends on experiments, precise observations, and where possible, measurements to test theories.

✓ Science is repeatable. A researcher gets similar results each time an experiment is done, and other researchers get similar results when they try those same experiments.

✓ Science evolves. Through experimentation and discovery, researchers replace old observations and theories with revised ones. This scientific method is the heart of science.

✓ Science insists that experiments and results are published in professional journals, where referees check them and other scientists can learn from them.

2 Science Watch

Keeping a watch on science means asking a lot of probing questions about who's doing research on what, how they are doing their research, and why they are doing it. To get you rolling, become familiar with the Baloney Busters listed here. They're designed to help you

CHALLENGE the research that scientists design and conduct,

ANALYZE the analysis they do on the research results, and

QUESTION the conclusions they arrive at.

There are more questions you can ask, but consider these a starter kit that you can use whenever you come across reports about science. Ask yourself whether the source of your information can answer all the questions. If it cannot, you might be able to contact the media who reported the research — and if possible, the scientists themselves. The easiest and quickest way to reach them is through e-mail and the Internet. If you can't get any clear answers or the information just doesn't seem to be there, it's best not to trust the research.

Challenge the Research

Everyone from your mother to the guy who runs the local ice cream shop tells stories about Cousin Jake's method for locating underground water — how he shows up in a bright red jacket and yellow rubber boots and how he always whistles "On Top of Old Smokey" while holding a bent coat hanger in front of him. These stories might spur an idea for research, but they're certainly not evidence to support Jake's water-finding method. For instance, they don't tell you whether or not other people could do the same things and find water, how many of Jake's water-finding efforts failed (like everybody, he's more likely to recall hits than misses), and how many of his successes were due solely to chance. For that, you need sound research done by qualified scientists who design and conduct good studies. Make sure that is what's backing up scientific research before you rely on it.

BALONEY BUSTER 1

Wearing the Wrong Hat

You've been going to an excellent dentist, Dr. Whitegrin, for several years. She's always checked your teeth, filled any cavities, and given you fluoride treatments. One day she tells you she's decided to test a new toothpaste, called SmileRite. She hands you and four other patients several tubes and asks you to use the toothpaste until you return for your next six-month checkup. Then she'll see how well SmileRite protects teeth from decay.

The problem is that being a dentist is very different from being a dental-health researcher. Like most people,

Dr. Whitegrin has had little training in research methods. For instance, she doesn't know how to set up experiments, how many people to test, how to analyze the results, or what to compare them with. What's more, when people like Dr. Whitegrin try to do research — even on subjects closely linked to their fields — they're probably not aware of the mistakes they're making.

ALWAYS ASK:
Were the researchers specifically trained to do research?

Big Buck Power

How do you feel when you hear that research into tooth decay was paid for by a candy company? or that a study of nutrition in plums was sponsored by a fruit growers' association? Suspicious? You should be. If scientists aren't careful, their research can be influenced by the company or association that's paying the bills. Think of the pressure on the researchers running the tests to prove that a new type of candy did not contribute to cavities or that plums were especially nutritious. What happens is not usually an intentional fudging of results, but pressure to come up with a particular conclusion can easily cause research errors that bias the findings.

"In all my years as a science editor, the trap I worried about most was the one set by scientists who saw themselves as advocates for one point of view or another."

— Richard Flaste, science editor

As governments and universities find fewer and fewer dollars to fund research, scientists are increasingly turning to companies and associations for money. You can't toss out all the research that's supported by someone with a stake in the results, but you certainly have the right to know who paid for the work. And you can ask what researchers did to make sure the results weren't influenced by the opinions of the funders.

ALWAYS ASK:
Who funded the research? Could the research have been affected by the point of view of the funder?

Be especially wary of scientists who become spokespersons for corporations or special causes. They are often paid to promote particular points of view and may frown on any research that disagrees with the official company line. Scientists employed by a cigarette manufacturer, for instance, might find it hard to be objective about research showing that nicotine in cigarettes is addictive.

BALONEY BUSTER 3 — Trash Is Trash — Published or Not

To break the summer boredom, your kid brother and his buddy are writing *The Neighborhood News,* a one-page newsletter describing who's doing what on your street. They report that the blackberries Mr. Peabody grows are good for treating bouts of flu. Of course, you wouldn't call *The Neighborhood News* a reliable source, but if you read about blackberries as a flu treatment in a newspaper, magazine, or Internet site, you might be tempted to try them when you're sick.

Popular sources of information publish both good and bad science. Before you start tossing back blackberries, you'd be wise to find out if research into their treatment value had ever been published in a professional scientific journal.

(The media often refer to scientific journals in their articles.) Then you'd know whether or not the research had been screened by a team of scientists and had met the standards set by the journals. Of course, some scientific journals are more careful and demanding than others, but their checking process is one line of defense against bad science. And that's one line more than newspapers, popular magazines, and Internet sites offer. What's more, many scientific journals — including all medical journals — require researchers to reveal any involvement they have with companies or individuals who have a stake in the results of the studies.

ALWAYS ASK: Was the research published in a professional scientific journal?

Mind the Medical Mouse

Sick? Worried? Looking for a cure? A few clicks of a mouse and you're bound to find an answer. Well, you're sure to find advice at any rate. What it's worth is another matter. Medical Web sites — about 100 000 of them — offer a huge range of information on illnesses, therapies, medicines, and more, but many sites are misleading or plain dishonest.

Anybody can post information on the Internet and claim just about anything. There are no checks. Sites that are full of dubious information can look and sound highly scientific, so it can be tricky to tell the good ones from the bad. At the very least, see if a site offers up-to-date data supported by scientific research. Find out who set up the site and who is providing the information. Check its reputation with health watchdog sites, such as Quackwatch.

http://www.quackwatch.com

BALONEY BUSTER 4

When a Duck Is Not a Duck

Now you might assume researchers would know what on earth they're studying — but not all of them do. Take geologist Georgia. She wants to research floods — where and when they occur and what contributes to them — but she doesn't have a clear idea of what she's calling a "flood." Is it simply water that has spilled over onto land? Okay, but if it's only a trickle of water, is it a flood? If it lasts for just an hour, is it a flood? If it doesn't do any damage — in fact, if it does some good, as it does in a rice field — is it still a flood?

Georgia doesn't have to come up with a definition to end all definitions. She just has to be clear and consistent about what she's studying in that particular piece of research. Otherwise, what use are her observations and conclusions?

> ALWAYS ASK:
> Did the researchers clearly define what they studied?

Far better are the researchers hired by your school board to study the high rate of unexcused student absenteeism in the district. They started by defining absenteeism — "at least two hours missed from a scheduled school session without a written excuse acceptable to the school principal and signed by the student's legal guardian." A specific definition like that is one of the first steps in setting up a quality study.

Your Turn

Even something as "obvious" as traffic deaths needs defining before it can be researched. Find out how your health department, highway department, coroner's office, local and regional police departments, and insurance companies define road traffic deaths. Do some definitions include only victims found dead on the road, while others also count those who died in hospitals within a week? a month? a year? What about people with traffic injuries that later led to death by heart attacks or pneumonia? If a helicopter crashed on the highway, would the deaths of its occupants count as road traffic deaths? Imagine the confusion if researchers comparing the road traffic deaths in two cities relied on local police reports that used different definitions.

So, Who's Everybody?

You can never study all the elephants in the world nor all the jeans made in a factory. That's why scientists select individual elephants and jeans to test, then use the test results to make judgments about them all. The individuals chosen (the sample) are selected from all the elephants or jeans available (the population). This works well as long as the samples are a lot like the population.

First, scientists have to decide exactly what population they're going to research. Suppose they're setting up a study of elephants. There are two species of elephants in the world: the big-eared African elephants and the smaller-eared Asian ones. Is the research population for this study going to be all elephants of both species? just Asian elephants? only Asian elephants that live in the wild? or just male Asian elephants that are at least five years old? You get the idea. If researchers aren't very clear about what population they're focusing on, they can't choose a sample that represents it.

ALWAYS ASK:
Exactly what population was researched?

23

A Chip off the Block — or Not

Good researchers draw samples that give every subject in the population a chance to be picked. They often use computers to pick the samples randomly from lists. A random sample of all Asian elephants, for instance, would include those living in the wild, in logging camps, in zoos, and more.

Samples that don't represent the population are called "biased." Suppose researchers studied only Asian elephants trained to do work, such as moving heavy logs. Results would show that almost every one of them can understand orders given by people — "Lift." "Drop it." "Sit." — which certainly isn't true of all Asian elephants. But biased samples aren't usually that obvious. For instance, if a sample was taken when a new batch of elephants had just arrived at a logging camp for training, researchers might conclude — wrongly — that Asian elephants are unable to understand people's commands.

Human subjects can create other kinds of sampling problems. To test a new cold remedy, for example, researchers can't choose a random sample of people with the sniffles and force them to take part. Many of them might not feel like getting out of bed. Those who volunteer for the study might be suffering their ninth cold that year and feel absolutely desperate to find a cure — which can bias test results.

You should also be wary of polls that use self-selected samples, such as the ones a newspaper holds when it asks readers to send in their opinions. These samples are almost always biased. They tend to include only people who are passionate enough about the topic to respond — and, of course, only those who read that particular newspaper. If a paper polled the public about whether or not the city should require cats to be walked on leashes, imagine the outcry from cat owners. But the same people might not bother to respond to a poll on banning beach volleyball.

ALWAYS ASK: Did the sample represent the population?

BALONEY BUSTER — *Size Matters*

If you check just one, two, or three pairs of jeans made in a factory, you can say little about the quality of all the jeans made there. So how many jeans should you check? That's a tough question because there are no strict rules about sample size. But bigger is usually better — especially when test subjects might vary a lot.

The strength and colorfastness of jeans in a large sample are probably representative of the strength and colorfastness of all the jeans made in the factory.

ALWAYS ASK: Was the sample large enough?

Be suspicious of studies based on very small samples. At best, they might suggest a focus for more research — but that's all.

Your Turn

How much wood could a woodchuck chuck if a woodchuck would chuck wood? To tackle this well-known riddle, two researchers from Harvard Medical School stuck 12 male adult woodchucks in a cage and fed them wood for two weeks. Their conclusion? *"Marmota monax* is able to chuck wood at a rate of 361.9237001 cubic centimeters [22.0859393 cubic inches] per day." Given this information, choose the statement(s) that you agree with:

(a) The sample size is too small.

(b) The sample doesn't include females and young woodchucks, who may not chuck wood or who may chuck wood at a rate different from that of male adult woodchucks.

(c) Some scientists have a sense of humor.

(d) All of the above.

(Check "Solutions," page 100.)

Control Needed

Suppose you heard that people who use medicated Clear-It-Up face cream get 50% fewer pimples. "Than who?" you should holler. Poor researchers wouldn't have a solid answer. But good researchers would have tested a control group — people who are similar to the test subjects in age, gender, lifestyle, and so on. Unknown to them, these control subjects would have been using Clear-It-Up face cream that contained no medication. Then if the test subjects got 50% fewer pimples than the control subjects, researchers could say the difference might be linked to the medication in Clear-It-Up.

ALWAYS ASK: Was a control group used?

Control groups are needed for many kinds of research, but they are not used nearly as much as they should be. That's often why phony healers falsely declare a high rate of success for their treatments. Dr. Quacksalot may claim he cures 75% of his patients' headaches by rubbing their hair, but without proper research and a control group, he can't prove his treatment is better than any other — or than no treatment at all.

Setting the Stage

Having a party? Invite 2 OR 20 friends. Light a fire and put out a selection of movie videos OR shove the furniture aside and turn on the music. The number of people you involve, the setting you arrange, and the activities you provide create the kind of party you'll have.

Setting the stage for research affects outcomes, too. Rats kept in a dark room then suddenly placed under bright lights, for instance, may grope around and find their way through a maze differently from rats held in normally lit rooms. And people tested on their responses to music may react differently depending on whether there's loud background noise or not. Careful design and control of study conditions help researchers get more accurate results.

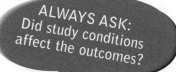

ALWAYS ASK:
Did study conditions affect the outcomes?

BALONEY BUSTER 10: Letting the Cat out of the Bag

A researcher can alter results by letting test subjects know what's expected of them. Suppose Susie Scientist is investigating the effects of eating carrots for breakfast. If Susie asked her subjects to report side effects, such as thirst, they would probably

Light Up Your Work — or Your Life?

Something strange was happening at a factory where scientists were studying the effects of lighting levels. When they brightened the place, the workers became more productive. As the lighting levels were raised again and again, the employees in the factory worked harder and harder. But when the scientists started to lower the lights, the workers worked — not less — but more. Each time the light levels dropped, production in the factory climbed higher. In fact, it didn't start to fall until the lights were so dim the workers could barely see.

Finally, the scientists realized that the workers had been responding, not to the changes in lighting, but to the extra attention they were getting throughout the study.

Your Turn See if you can affect people's behavior with your voice alone. Put some raisins in two small bowls, and pass one bowl around, saying, "Try these raisins." Then pass the second bowl, saying the same thing, but snickering slightly as you say "these." People may not be as willing to try the raisins from the second bowl.

"notice" they were thirsty. Just the suggestion that eating carrots at breakfast increases thirst is enough to make some subjects feel like drinking.

Even subtle clues — a raised eyebrow, a grin, or a change in tone of voice — can influence study results. If Susie is testing pink pain pills, she might also give her research subjects yellow pills that do nothing to ease pain. Any hint from Susie that the yellow pills are fakes can affect how people react to both sets of pills. Susie would be wise to use an assistant — someone who knows nothing about the pills — to hand them out and collect information about their effects. In research, that's called a "double-blind technique" — neither the assistant nor the subjects know what to expect from the experiment.

ALWAYS ASK: Did the researchers have opportunities to influence the results?

11 Questionable Questions

Have you stopped beating your dog? Answer either "yes" or "no" and you sound cruel. But probably the truth is that you have never beaten your dog or that you don't even own a dog. When researchers ask poor questions, they get worthless answers. And there are so many kinds of poor questions. Here are just a few.

UNANSWERABLE QUESTIONS: "Does your family like your neighbors?" You can't speak for all the members of your family. Besides, your family may like some — but not all — of the neighbors.

VAGUE QUESTIONS: "Do you think young people today have a wide range of opportunities?" You're left wondering which young people, what kind of opportunities (educational, entertainment, job, travel, or others), and how many opportunities make up a "wide range"?

BIASED QUESTIONS: "Do you agree with the Pope's idea to hold a world conference on gun control?" Your answer might be influenced by knowing that the idea came from a famous and powerful person.

SILENT-ALTERNATIVE QUESTIONS: "Do you think employers who fill part-time jobs with students and lay them off during slow seasons should arrange to provide year-round part-time jobs for students?" You might answer differently if you knew the unspoken alternative — that employers might pay lower wages so they could afford to provide these year-round jobs.

ALWAYS ASK: Were research questions carefully worded?

BALONEY 12 BUSTER Questioning Questionable Questions

Besides wording questions carefully, good researchers avoid asking poor questions through pretesting — trying out the questions on a sample of people similar to the test subjects. After a pretest, the researchers discuss the questions with the people who answered them. The object is to learn which questions were too hard, too confusing, or too limiting. That information helps the researchers pinpoint questions that should be reworded, dropped, or added.

Here are some examples of questions before pretesting and the changes that might result. Unfortunately, poor researchers seldom pretest their questions, so they don't catch problems before they carry out their studies.

BEFORE PRETEST

Do you ever watch hockey and soccer on TV?

Like most people your age, do you watch TV documentaries only rarely?

About how much time do you spend watching TV in a normal week?

What impact has TV had on your family?

PROBLEM

Combining two questions.

Biased.

No problem.

Unanswerable. Respondent can't say how TV affects each individual.

AFTER PRETEST

Do you ever watch hockey on TV?
Do you ever watch soccer on TV?

How often do you usually watch TV documentaries?
- frequently?
- occasionally?
- rarely?
- never?

No change is needed.

Drop the question.

ALWAYS ASK: Were the questions pretested?

Your Turn

Try your own question pretest. Ask some of your friends the unanswerable question and the vague question in Baloney Buster #11, and see what kinds of responses you get. Then ask your friends why they had a tough time answering.

BALONEY 13 BUSTER

Half-truths

Gather just half the facts and you have just half the story. Based on accident reports received by insurance companies, a study of car collisions may turn up more teenaged drivers than middle-aged drivers. But has the study got all the data it needs? Unlike teenagers, middle-aged drivers can often afford to pay for their own repairs. They may choose not to report accidents that make their insurance costs rise. A study of car collisions might have to look beyond insurance company records to get the rest of the story.

Even when researchers try hard to track down all the data they need, something important can easily slip by. Think how one test subject must have affected a diet study by reporting she'd barely lost any weight although she'd had only boiled eggs and coffee for several weeks. When questioned further, she admitted putting "two sugars" in her coffee. Oh, yes ... and she drank 60 cups a day!

ALWAYS ASK: Were the data complete?

Your Turn

Suppose you want to compare the auto safety records of student drivers trained by Steer Rite School with those of student drivers trained by Wheel On School. You compare the statistics and see that, after one year, Steer Rite grads have twice as many accidents as Wheel On grads. Can you claim that Wheel On grads are safer?

If you discovered that Steer Rite drivers drove twice as far and during twice as many snowstorms as Wheel On drivers in the same time period, might you change your mind?

BALONEY BUSTER 14

Wishes Don't Make It Right

Wishes don't often come true, but in research, they sometimes influence results. Scientists are only human, so they might unintentionally ignore data that don't support their theories, or they might pay more attention to data that do. Rotten researchers often do the same thing on purpose. It's an error known as "data dredging."

Researchers who think dreams can predict the future, for instance, may focus on the few dreams that coincidentally "came true" and ignore the many that didn't. For instance, if you found a stray poodle in your yard a few months after dreaming of playing with a curly-haired puppy under a tree, dream researcher Ricko might say, "Didn't I tell you so?" But he says nothing about your dream of escaping from a burning building and hundreds of other dreams that failed to predict anything in your life.

ALWAYS ASK: Were the data considered fairly?

Do You See What I See?

Eight years after the discovery of X-rays in 1895, French physicist Prosper René Blondlot claimed to have discovered an invisible radiation that he called N-rays. He said N-rays brightened any flash of electric light they passed through.

Using a special viewing apparatus centering on a prism made of aluminum, Blondlot claimed he could bend N-rays to produce a spectrum — much like you use a glass prism to bend light and produce bands of colors. Several of Blondlot's colleagues in France reported the same results.

Along came a doubting American physicist, Robert Wood. He and other scientists outside France had failed to locate any of the so-called N-rays using Blondlot's methods, so he decided to visit the French lab for a demonstration. Blondlot set up the viewing apparatus in a dark room and started describing what he was "observing." Wood still couldn't see a thing, so he made his move. Secretly, he slipped the prism out of the viewing apparatus, but Blondlot continued to describe the spectrum. After Wood published the results of his visit, the notion of N-rays quickly disappeared.

Analyze the Analysis

Scientists calculate figures called "statistics" to describe and analyze their research findings. The trouble is that statistics — even simple ones, such as averages — can be massaged and misused to support almost any conclusion. You don't have to be a statistician or any other kind of mathematician to quiz scientists about an analysis they've done. Just practice safe stats by asking questions.

Get Rich Scheme

"Choose the gender of your future child! Send $50 for Baby Boy Pills or Baby Girl Pills. Results guaranteed — or your money back." People with little understanding of statistics might be taken in by this ad. Most women have about as much chance of giving birth to a boy as to a girl, so the pills don't need to do anything at all. The shady dealer can keep about half of the money received — all for the cost of advertising and some worthless sugar pills. What a profit!

Which Average Joe?

There's not just one way to describe what's average, there are three.

MEAN OR ARITHMETICAL AVERAGE: It's the sum of all the figures divided by the number of figures.

MEDIAN: It's the midpoint. When figures are listed in order of value, half the figures fall at or below this midpoint, and half fall at or above. If there is an even number of figures, the median is the mean of the two middle figures.

MODE: Of all the figures in a list, it's the one that occurs most frequently.

Suppose Ruffy the Rat was learning to run a maze. The scores — out of 10 — that Ruffy earned are listed below:

Run 1: 3   Run 2: 4   Run 3: 5   Run 4: 3   Run 5: 10

You can quickly spot the mode, the most frequent score: 3. And it's easy to figure out Ruffy's median score — the midpoint. First, list all the scores in order of value:

Run 1: 3   Run 4: 3   Run 2: 4   Run 3: 5   Run 5: 10

Now pick out the score that falls in the middle: 4. Both the mode (3) and the median (4) give Ruffy a failing average. But what if you calculate the mean? Add the scores (25), then divide by the number of scores (5), and you end up with 5 —

Did you hear the average joke about the sharks who were schooled in statistics? One lunged and missed a swimmer by 30 cm (12 in.) to the right. Another lunged and missed a swimmer by 30 cm (12 in.) to the left. "Yummy!" they hollered. "We've got swimmer for dinner."

a passing average. If researchers are anxious to make Ruffy look good, they will report only the mean and not mention the median or the mode.

In a second group of tests, the same researchers — still trying to impress you with Ruffy's smarts — might report only the median. Suppose the rat got these scores:

Run 6: 1   Run 7: 1   Run 8: 5   Run 9: 6   Run 10: 7

The mode (1) and the mean (20 ÷ 5 = 4) are both failing averages. But the median (5) gives Ruffy a passing average. In this set of runs, the researchers might choose to report only the median.

ALWAYS ASK: Were all the averages reported?

To form the clearest picture of any research results, it's best to see all the averages: mean, median, and mode.

Your Turn   **You arrive** home with your report card and your knees are knocking. Your math grade really hit your average hard. That is, it hit your mean (69%) hard. Look at your grades and see how much smarter you'll appear if you announce your average only as the median.

(Check "Solutions," page 100.)

English: 86%
French: 82%
Social Studies: 80%
Biology: 70%
Math: 28%

BALONEY 16 BUSTER

Rank Isn't Everything

You might be impressed to hear your history mark was in the 95th percentile of all the history marks in your class. That means the history marks of 95% of all the other students were equal to or lower than yours. But you'd be less impressed if you knew that all those history marks — including yours — were lower than a C. That's the trouble with percentiles. Just like medians — which are 50th percentiles — they fail to give you any idea of the value of each percentile.

Researchers who report results only as percentiles might be trying to pull the wool over your eyes — hoping you'll assume what they want you to. Suppose a water-quality study of 10 lakes revealed that your local watering hole, Murky Lake, ranked in the 90th percentile. Sounds good, but if 8 of the lakes were actually below acceptable standards, you might not want to spend your summer swimming at Murky Lake. You'd need to find out just how much better it ranked than the other lakes.

ALWAYS ASK: Were results hidden in percentiles?

Your Turn

Your friend Beth is trying to convince her parents to raise her allowance. Help her argue for a raise by showing her how to report her weekly allowance as a percentile of the allowances she and nine of her friends receive — even though there's not much difference in the amounts. What percentile does Beth's allowance fall into?

	Weekly Allowance
Jan	$15.00
Tom	$15.00
Carlo	$15.00
Sara	$15.00
Kathy	$15.00
Jerry	$15.00
Steve	$15.00
Beth	$14.50
You	$14.50
Mike	$14.00

(Check "Solutions," page 100.)

BALONEY BUSTER 17

False Illusion

Research results figured to several decimal points, such as 2.90763, can look precise — even impressive. So some researchers try to make a study appear more accurate than it really is by calculating more decimal points than the data deserve. If the data consist only of rough estimates, precise calculations are plain silly. You wouldn't take the approximate lengths (nose to tail) of three dogs — 86, 96, and 110 cm (34, 38, and 43 in.) — and report their mean length as 97.333333 cm (38.333333 in.).

A woman moved to a city of 97 000 people. As she arrived, she stopped by the road into town and changed a sign to read "Population: 97 001."

Suppose a study of skateboard sales in your community found that five store managers estimated selling about 12, 5, 20, 10, and 2 skateboards every month. Concluding that the mean monthly sale per store was 9.8 skateboards is unrealistically accurate because the sales figures were only approximate in the first place. The results of a study can never be more exact than the data that go into it.

Converting figures from metric to imperial and vice versa can create some meaningless measurements, too. If one number has been rounded off — say to a mile — it doesn't make sense to convert it to 1.609 kilometers. A better conversion would be "about 1.5 kilometers."

> **ALWAYS ASK:**
> Were the data as precise as the calculations?

For years, the normal temperature of the human body was considered to be 98.6° Fahrenheit — or close to it. After millions of healthy body temperatures were checked, that figure was corrected to 98.2°. Why was the first figure inaccurate? Originally, the temperature had been figured in Celsius and rounded off to 37°, but the rounding was forgotten when the figure was later converted to Fahrenheit.

BALONEY BUSTER 18 — Crowns Don't Make Kings

Physicist T. D. Lee sometimes grabbed lunch at a restaurant close to Columbia University, New York. The day after he won a Nobel Prize in 1957, the restaurant manager posted a sign in the window: "Eat here, win Nobel Prize." You may laugh, but the manager's actions illustrate what many people — including weak researchers — sometimes do. When they spot a relationship between two things, they assume one caused the other.

George wolfed down 10 kg (22 lb.) of apples and a single cherry in one day — and got sick. The next day he ate the same amount of bananas and a cherry and got sick. He ate the same amount of oranges and a cherry the third day and got sick again. Dr. Flimflam concluded, "It must have been the cherry!"

When good scientists examine a relationship between things — called a "correlation" — they're checking to see if changes in one usually accompany changes in the other. Suppose they found that people who ate Peppi's Hot Dogs suffered sneezing fits. The more they ate, the more they sneezed. Scientists might say there's a correlation between eating Peppi's Hot Dogs and sneezing. They'd also check to see if that correlation depended on something that was linked to both sneezing and eating Peppi's Hot Dogs. Sour pickles, perhaps. It's possible that, if people didn't eat sour pickles with their Peppi's Hot Dogs, there would be no correlation between eating the hot dogs and sneezing.

Still, scientists cannot conclude that sour pickles cause sneezing. For that, they'd have to do a lot more research, and they might use one of two approaches.

- They might look for what's common among things related to an event: If an acid that's in sour

Sewage Links

In 1829, many people in London, England, were dying from cholera, an illness usually marked by extreme diarrhea. A city official named William Farr studied the problem by looking at the patients' occupations, incomes, and housing. The only link he found to cholera was this: the closer people lived to the River Thames, the more likely they were to get this dreaded disease. So far, so good — except that Farr blamed the smelly, polluted air rising from the river for causing cholera.

It wasn't until 1853 that English physician John Snow discovered something else that correlated with both cholera and the river: the sewers that emptied into the Thames. People who lived near the greatest concentrations of sewage drank the most polluted water — and ran the greatest risk of getting cholera. When the sewage disposal system improved, cholera almost completely disappeared from London.

Nibbling on Einstein's Brain

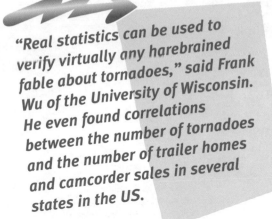

"Real statistics can be used to verify virtually any harebrained fable about tornadoes," said Frank Wu of the University of Wisconsin. He even found correlations between the number of tornadoes and the number of trailer homes and camcorder sales in several states in the US.

pickles is also in several other foods that are linked to sneezing, then that acid might be a cause.

- Or they might look for what's different among things related to an event: Suppose scientists set up two identical batches of sour pickles and other foods linked to sneezing, but one batch contained pickles that lacked the suspect acid. If scientists found a link only between sneezing and eating the batch of food containing this acid, the acid might be a cause.

ALWAYS ASK: Was cause confused with correlation?

In either case, scientists would also do a statistical analysis to see if the "cause" might be happening only by chance. But good scientists would never confuse cause with correlation.

Did you hear about the scientist who experimented with a trained flea? He removed one pair of legs and said, "Jump." The flea jumped. He removed a second pair of legs and said, "Jump." The flea jumped. When the scientist removed the last pair of legs and said, "Jump," the flea stayed still. The scientist concluded, "When a flea loses all its legs, it becomes deaf."

Question the Conclusions

After scientists complete an analysis, they draw conclusions based on the results. At least, that's what they're supposed to do. Some researchers, however, conclude things that don't really reflect the findings of their research. So put Baloney Busters to work here, too.

BALONEY 19 BUSTER
Back That Up!

Good researchers present their results clearly and completely, and demonstrate how they draw their conclusions. But it's not unusual to find weak or phony researchers hiding results to support the points they want to make. Suppose a survey of a sample of high school students found that:

- 6% ranked Shiniest Ever as a great shampoo,
- 5% called it okay,
- 36% said it was terrible, and
- 53% had never used it.

Less-than-honest researchers might report, "Only 36% of the students surveyed didn't like Shiniest Ever," letting the reader assume that the rest of the students liked the shampoo.

What if you tried to get away with that kind of trick? Suppose only 1 of your 10 closest friends had a great time at Slippery Slope Ski Lodge, 6 had never been, and 3 didn't like it at all. Would you expect to convince your parents to let you go to the lodge by arguing, "Well, only 3 of my 10 best friends didn't like Slippery Slope Ski Lodge"?

ALWAYS ASK: Were the results abused to force a conclusion?

Your Turn

You hate cabbage, so you want to convince your folks to let you toss out most of the heads they picked from the vegetable garden. You check over the 10 they brought in and find that 6 have been attacked by something — bugs or fungus or both. Here's the breakdown.

- Cabbages attacked by bugs only: 2.
- Cabbages attacked by a fungus only: 2.
- Cabbages attacked by both bugs and a fungus: 2.

If you were sneaky, you could do something that researchers sometimes do — double-count. How could you report the damage to your parents so they'd conclude you should toss out 8 cabbages instead of just 6?

(Check "Solutions," page 100.)

Keep on Topic

Analyze water, and you can make conclusions about water — not about milk, orange juice, or hot chocolate. Careful scientists draw conclusions only about the population or sample they have studied. If a large sample of rats responded to the sound of Elvis Presley's singing by eating faster, scientists might conclude that other rats would likely react the same way. But could they conclude listening to Elvis would have the same effect on rabbits, deer, or people? Their reactions would need to be tested individually in other experiments.

Did you hear about the researchers who concluded three-quarters of all people were born in France? They surveyed 10 000 people living in Paris.

ALWAYS ASK:
Did the conclusions overstep?

Picture This

Some researchers wrap up their reports with graphs that summarize their findings. The graphs may appear to support their conclusions, but they can easily mislead you.

For instance, Gloria Gardener developed a new type of tomato plant called Terrific Tomatoes. She tested her plant and two other kinds — Rosy Tomatoes and Juicy Tomatoes — and plotted her findings on a graph.

At first glance, the graph appears to support Gloria's conclusion, which says, "Terrific Tomatoes are the best kind to grow," but check again. The graph doesn't give you any idea what "Growth" means — speed of growth, height of plants, size of tomatoes, whatever. There are no numbers to indicate time, height, or weight.

Now look over the graphs that Richard Researcher sketched. He will select one of them for his report on raccoon feedings times.

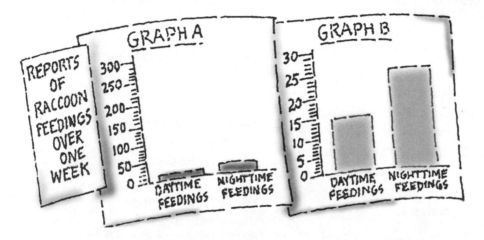

Watch for graphs in your local newspaper. Clip them out — along with the articles they illustrate — and check them over to see how clear and fair they are. Think what you might do to improve them.

Even though both graphs show the same thing, the difference between the number of times raccoons were seen feeding during the day (15) and during the night (25) appears to be greater in graph B. That's because graph B is marked off in units of 1; graph A, in units of 10. If Richard has concluded that raccoons feed significantly more often at night, he will likely decide to include graph B in his report. That graph seems to support his conclusion better than graph A does.

ALWAYS ASK: Did the graphs summarize the research findings clearly and fairly?

◆ ◆ ◆

Now that you've discovered ways to challenge scientific research, analyze the analysis of its results, and question the conclusions drawn, you're well on your way to sifting the bad science from the good. Remember: the more you keep a watch on science, the better at it you become. Refer often to the summary checklist provided here — and bust that baloney!

Baloney Buster Checklist

CHALLENGE THE RESEARCH

1. Were the researchers specifically trained to do research?
2. Who funded the research? Could the research have been affected by the point of view of the funder?
3. Was the research published in a professional scientific journal?
4. Did the researchers clearly define what they studied?
5. Exactly what population was researched?
6. Did the sample represent the population?
7. Was the sample large enough?
8. Was a control group used?
9. Did study conditions affect the outcomes?
10. Did the researchers have opportunities to influence the results?
11. Were research questions carefully worded?
12. Were the questions pretested?
13. Were the data complete?
14. Were the data considered fairly?

ANALYZE THE ANALYSIS

15. Were all the averages reported?
16. Were results hidden in percentiles?
17. Were the data as precise as the calculations?
18. Was cause confused with correlation?

QUESTION THE CONCLUSIONS

19. Were the results abused to force a conclusion?
20. Did the conclusions overstep?
21. Did the graphs summarize the research findings clearly and fairly?

3 Media Watch

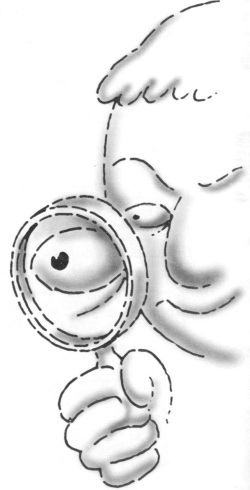

Get real! How many people ever read professional scientific journals or have researchers at their elbows to keep them informed about science? Like almost everybody else, you probably rely on the media — TV, radio, newspapers, magazines, books, and the Internet — to learn about advances in science. So it's lucky there are professional reporters and even some advertisers who do a good job filling you in.

Unfortunately, not all media people do their job well. They might not report some of the science you need to know, or they might not report it thoroughly, clearly, or fairly. Many people who work in the media struggle — just as much as you do — to understand science. That's why it's important to maintain a watch on the media, using Media Alerts such as the ones listed here. They'll help you

REVIEW the reporting of scientific research and its results, and

CRITIQUE the ads that use research results to persuade you to buy products and services.

As you get the hang of it, you'll likely come up with some Media Alerts of your own.

Review the Reporting

In centuries past, town criers took the news from town to town, shouting it out to crowds gathered on street corners. If a crier got his facts wrong, he would muddle some of the minds of the day, but he wouldn't affect masses of people.

Consider how times have changed. With today's communications technology, a single news report can circle the globe almost instantly, reaching millions of people. So when reporters muddle science news, they do a disservice to the world. Be on the alert.

1 *A Little Isn't Enough*

Give reporters a minute or two behind a microphone — or a single column in a newspaper — and they can't possibly do a thorough job of presenting a scientific study. They often skip to the conclusions without offering any details to help you judge the quality of the research and the results. Who funded the research? What was the sample size? How was the study done? How do the results compare with other research on this subject?

"The assumption that people have no patience for difficult concepts...is a self-fulfilling prophecy."

— Catherine Ford, newspaper columnist

Too often reporters don't devote enough space to science news because they assume people won't absorb the details. But that's a weak argument. If reporters never present the whole story, then the public can't become interested in it.

It's your right to know more about the science that affects you, your health, and your lifestyle. Before you charge off to the drugstore to buy the latest reported "cure" for headaches, you need to know how well you can rely on the research behind it.

ALWAYS ASK: Was the research reported adequately?

MEDIA ALERT

2 *Clear as Mud*

Even facts that are well researched and accurately reported can mislead the public if they're not well explained. Suppose, for instance, that some dreaded disease attacks one person in ten. On hearing that, people might immediately assume that they have a one in ten chance of dying from this disease, not just of getting it. Or they might think that the rate of developing the disease is the same for people of all ages when, in fact, it increases as people age. It's a reporter's responsibility to head off confusion.

Your Turn

Watch your local newspaper and collect headlines that could confuse readers. Here's one that's just plain funny: "Robotic 'Doctors' Operate on Batteries."

Putting research into a bigger picture, or context, also helps people understand it better. For instance, the risk of getting a particular disease may appear to have increased over time, but better methods of diagnosing it might account for part of that increase. So might the fact that more people are living longer and reaching an age when the risk of getting this disease is greater.

ALWAYS ASK: Was the research explained well?

MEDIA ALERT 3

Talking the Talk

"Blah, blah, blah.... And Dr. Pribble found appreciable reductions in radial incremental growth as a result of...blah, blah, blah." Say that again! Some reporters simply talk the talk. They might not understand the research they're reporting well enough to translate it into plain English. Or they might prefer to use technical words — "jargon" — because they think it makes their reporting sound more impressive or credible. Either way, they're not serving the public well because they're not presenting information in words people easily understand. For instance, one reporter praised the use of "vertical landscape design features" (trees). Another referred to "in-class facilitators of pupil learning" (teachers). To be fair, many scientists have trouble talking about their research in non-technical language. Still, it's a reporter's job to learn the meaning of the jargon.

Your Turn

Try your hand at turning gobbledygook into plain English. Can you reduce this sentence to just three words? "The utilization of standing devices made of wood and wire eliminates the meandering of populations of bovines."

(Check "Solutions," page 100.)

ALWAYS ASK: Did the reporter weed out the jargon?

vertical landscape design features...

in-class facilitators of pupil learning.

MEDIA ALERT 4

Backup Needed

A cure for AIDS? Contact with aliens? In the media's rush to report a major breakthrough, reporters may feature results from pioneer research before it's been repeated by other scientists. And sometimes scientists, impatient to get their work recognized, press the media for premature coverage.

Newspaper, TV, or radio reporters seldom caution their audiences that chance alone can create the results of a single study or that a study's design or methods can bias its results. Sometimes the media even use conclusions from a single, exploratory study as a reason to toss out long-established ideas — especially where food is concerned.

"The media are willing victims of bad information, and increasingly they are producers of it."

— Cynthia Crossen, reporter and editor

Newspapers reported one poorly conducted study that claimed eating a lot of white bread daily did not lead to weight gain and might even reduce weight. Sponsored by a major bread maker (see Baloney Buster #2: Big Buck Power), the research tested only 118 subjects, split into four groups — that's fewer than 30 people per group (see Baloney Buster #7: Size Matters). Here's how the study was designed.

GROUP A ate their usual meals.

GROUP B added four slices of low-calorie bread to their meals.

GROUP C added eight slices of low-calorie bread to their meals.

GROUP D added eight slices of regular bread to their meals.

ALWAYS ASK:
Did the reporter find other studies that backed up the research?

The study lasted only eight weeks — a short time for weight studies. Its conclusions? No one gained or lost weight, but the researchers said they thought subjects might have lost weight in a longer study. Hmm!

MEDIA ALERT 5 *Significant — Really?*

Now hear this: a local news team has uncovered a study of mean grades of schools in your town. They report a "significant difference" between the mean grade at your school and the mean grade at Lofty School. What's more, Lofty's mean is higher! But before you get all worked up about it, you need to know if the difference was truly significant or if it was what scientists call "statistically significant."

After they've completed their research, researchers run calculations to see if the result they got likely occurred by mere chance. If it didn't, they say that the result is statistically significant. But that doesn't mean the finding is necessarily an important one that has any practical significance. In fact, the mean grade at Lofty School (69.5%) was only 2.5% higher than the mean grade at your school (67%) — not much of a difference and certainly not a big enough difference to call it significant. In saying the study result was statistically significant, the researchers were simply stating that the difference between the mean grades likely didn't happen just by chance. But reporters who don't understand the statistical term often assume it means the same as significant. They can innocently mislead you into thinking something important has been discovered.

> **ALWAYS ASK:** Did the reporter confuse statistical significance with practical significance?

MEDIA ALERT 6 — *Wow Appeal!*

If a man can die, asleep in his own bed, when ice from an airplane crashes through his roof, it's hard to think of anything that's truly risk free. Yet reports of any risk tend to frighten people, and the media sometimes fan that fear. They can make risks sound worse than they really are. After all, sensational news sells!

Suppose, for instance, that researchers discovered Dozydrop candies increased the risk of fainting from 1 in 10 000 to 3 in 10 000. You might spot a headline that read, "Sucking Dozydrops Triples Risk of Fainting." True,

Your Turn

Suppose you switched on your radio to hear that 2000 was the "deadliest year in the history of airplanes" because a record number of passengers died during those 12 months. What kinds of information would you need to decide whether or not you agreed with the reporter's conclusion?

(Check "Solutions," page 100.)

but very misleading. If you did not know the actual, ridiculously low figures, you might avoid Dozydrops like poison.

Mathematician John Allen Paulos calculated that if you mixed one small jar full of a dangerous chemical with enough water to fill 2 600 000 000 000 000 000 000 small jars, the water in each jar would contain 6000 molecules of the chemical. No one would fear results that were reported as "Chemical in Water Equals 1 Part in 2 600 000 000 000 000 000 000." But expressing exactly the same results as "6000 Molecules of Chemical in Small Jar of Water" might terrify readers who don't understand how tiny that amount really is.

ALWAYS ASK: Was the research sensationalized?

MEDIA ALERT

7 Pick-and-choose Reporting

Reporters have the results of many studies and surveys at their fingertips. They draw from all this research to prepare their broadcasts or newspaper articles. If they're careful, responsible reporters, they'll write complete, well-balanced stories. If they're not, they'll pick out only the research results that support their particular points of view and skip over the rest.

ALWAYS ASK: Did the reporter sift research results to support a point of view?

Suppose an economics study of two toy factories showed that production of beach balls this year rose 5% in Fun Factory and just 2% in Joy Makers. Reporters would be wrong to claim that Fun Factory was more productive than Joy Makers if the same study also showed Fun Factory's production last year (90 000 beach balls) was 10% below Joy Maker's (100 000 beach balls).

MEDIA ALERT 8

Assumption — or Fact?

Around Squishville, motorists were spotting more dead porcupines than ever before — especially along roads through wooded areas. Reporter Rebecca got right on the story and found some recent wildlife studies showing that roadkill was on the rise. She wrote up her story and concluded: "Porcupine populations around Squishville have exploded." But that conclusion was likely based on her assumptions, not on the wildlife studies. Although it's possible that Rebecca was right, it's more probable that road expansion and increased traffic were responsible for the greater number of porcupine deaths. She should have checked out her story further.

> **ALWAYS ASK:** Are the conclusions based on the reporter's own assumptions?

MEDIA ALERT 9

Never-never Land

Ask a scientist to say "never" and her voice cracks. Even when there are hundreds of carefully conducted studies on a subject — all supporting one another's findings — scientists are seldom able to put words such as "never" or "always" in their conclusions. That's simply the nature of the beast called science, but it's something that the media — and the public — often forget or misunderstand.

Suppose researchers shone an unusual kind of light on thousands of monkeys for 18 hours a day, month after month for years, and found no more cancer among them than among monkeys who had never been exposed to this light. It would be amazing to find, later on, that the light was actually linked to cancer. But it is possible — so scientists can't say the link will never exist.

"Science is far from a perfect instrument of knowledge. It's just the best we have."

— Carl Sagan, astronomer

ALWAYS ASK: Did the reporter ignore research because it isn't 100% certain?

People who understand science are comfortable with this level of uncertainty. But it makes many others deeply distrustful. They may accept advice that's hit-or-miss from their friends, but from science, they wrongly expect answers that are 100% sure. One newspaper columnist wrote of her frustration with science for providing only limited explanations, then concluded that it is better to have "irrational heads" making decisions. That's a classic case of throwing out the baby with the bath water. Even though science can't provide all the answers, it certainly forecasts weather more reliably than tea leaf readings do, and it can assess your talents and aptitudes better than handwriting analyses can.

Critique the Ads

"Nothing refreshes you faster than Lipsmacking Lemonade." "Brighten your smile with Glitterface, the toothpaste that leaves your teeth whiter." "Enroll now: Fritzy's Flexing Fitness Club can help you develop the kind of body you want." Every day, you're bombarded with media ads, all trying to persuade you to buy this or do that. At best, they're entertaining and informative, providing helpful facts about products and services. At worst, they're annoying and deceptive. Oh, there are laws against ads that lie, but they're often hard to police. And some ads — though truthful — are carefully presented to mislead you about the "research" they're based on. It's up to you to critique them skeptically.

MEDIA ALERT 10 *Blind Trust*

If you dress like a doctor and act like a doctor, it doesn't necessarily mean you are a doctor. Yet some TV, magazine, and newspaper ads show professional-looking men and women in white coats raving about a product. "A medicine you can use with confidence," they say, holding up a flu remedy. "This is what I recommend." Companies that run ads like these aren't claiming to have a medical researcher as a spokesperson. But they're likely counting on you to think that's the case and buy their "medically approved" products.

And how about those ads that use well-known, respected people to speak for products or services? Just because A. Goalie is a great hockey player doesn't mean his opinions on the healthfulness of Rise-and-Shine Pineapple Juice are well founded. A product that resorts to having a famous person flog it probably offers little or nothing more than its competition.

ALWAYS ASK:
Do ads try to generate false trust?

Putting the Squeeze on Lemons

Tired of being fooled by advertising? Complain directly to the sponsors and report their advertising to regional and national consumer groups that bring poor advertising practices to the public's attention. Consumer groups headed by the Center for Science in the Public Interest in Washington, DC, for instance, embarrass companies that use questionable advertising by giving them Harlan Page Hubbard Lemon Awards. The lemon statues are named after a 19th-century charlatan who advertised a harmless but ineffective "medicine" called Lydia Pinkham's Vegetable Compound. It was sold as a cure for almost everything, including headaches, depression, indigestion — even cancer.

One Harlan Page Hubbard Lemon Award went to Quaker Oats' TV ads for telling only part of the story. During 1998, the ads claimed that eating Quaker oatmeal decreased cholesterol. But what they didn't mention was that eating oatmeal accounted for only about half the decrease among the people studied. Other changes in diet, plus exercise, accounted for the other half.

Ads for Ginsana — sold as an energy supplement — earned an award for ignoring scientific evidence. The ads declared Ginsana boosted energy, despite five published studies that failed to find any evidence to support the claim.

MEDIA ALERT 11 — Leading You On

You're stuck with washing the dishes again and you're not amused — even though Dad has tried to make life easier by providing "Sudsy, the Super Soap." As you struggle with a sticky casserole dish, the words from Sudsy's TV commercial burn in your ears: "No dish soap breaks down grease faster than Sudsy." In fact, it doesn't seem to work faster than any other soap you've tried. But does the commercial really say Sudsy is the fastest or does it just imply that — and count on you to think that's what is meant? In research tests, all brands of dish soap may have attacked grease just as fast as Sudsy — but not any faster.

Here's another approach to watch out for. Suppose an ad says, "Medical researchers rate AXC — the stomach-soothing ingredient in Feeling Jolly — as the best treatment for upset stomachs." The ad isn't claiming anything it shouldn't, even though all stomach-soothing medicines contain the ingredient AXC. But the advertisers may be hoping you'll assume AXC is found only in Feeling Jolly and buy their product.

ALWAYS ASK: Do ads imply more than the product research justifies?

Your Turn

One morning, your bossy brother holds up a box of breakfast food and reads, "Polly's Porridge is North America's Number One cereal." Then he shoves the box at you and says, "So eat it." How do you react?

(a) Tell your brother not to believe everything he reads — especially when it comes to advertising.

(b) Ask him to define "Number One cereal." Does it mean Polly's Porridge, is the best-selling cereal? the most nutritious? the most delicious? or what — exactly?

(c) Have him check the box for a toll-free phone number, call the makers of Polly's Porridge and ask why they call it "Number One" and how they back up their claim.

(d) All of the above.

(Check "Solutions," page 100.)

Search your kitchen for other items that claim to be great in one way or another and ask their manufacturers how they support what they say.

Fire Back

Companies may not lie about their products, but they sometimes make wild advertising claims to convince you to buy them. Don't assume these claims prove the products are marvelous. Instead, have some questions ready to fire at the companies, drawing on your Baloney Busters to help you. After all, a company's research of its own service or product is often simply bad research. To get you started, here are some examples of ad claims and how you might respond:

Wild Claims

Smart Comebacks

Tempting Treats contain 50% less fat.

Than what? whipped cream? competing products? the company's original Tempting Treats? (See Baloney Buster #8: Control Needed.)

Nine out of ten people who repair bikes recommend Speedy Wheels.

Did the survey include only people authorized to sell and repair Speedy Wheels and not other brands? How many people were surveyed? (See Baloney Busters #5: So, Who's Everybody?, #6: A Chip off the Block — or Not, and #7: Size Matters.)

One bowl of Zany cereal with milk supplies most of the nutrients you need.

How many nutrients come only or mostly from the milk? (See Baloney Buster #13: Half-truths)

In taste tests, 60% said Zing Juice was as good as or better than Zippy Juice.

What percentage said Zing was better and what percentage said Zippy was just as good? (See Baloney Buster #19: Back That Up!)

Leading magazines report that the pesticide in Free-of-Fleas is safe for your puppy.

Which "leading magazines"? Are they professional scientific journals? If not, do they use pesticide information that's backed by these journals? (See Baloney Buster #3: Trash Is Trash — Published or Not.)

◆ ◆ ◆

Okay, you're catching on. You've got your guard up, and you're watching how science is presented in the media — both in reporting and in advertising. Keep it up and you can do a lot to strengthen your skills in sorting the good science from the bad. This summary checklist is a reminder of the kinds of questions that will help you stay alert every time you encounter research in the media.

Media Alert Checklist

REVIEW THE REPORTING

1. Was the research reported adequately?
2. Was the research explained well?
3. Did the reporter weed out the jargon?
4. Did the reporter find other studies that backed up the research?
5. Did the reporter confuse statistical significance with practical significance?
6. Was the research sensationalized?
7. Did the reporter sift research results to support a point of view?
8. Are the conclusions based on the reporter's own assumptions?
9. Did the reporter ignore research because it isn't 100% certain?

CRITIQUE THE ADS

10. Do ads try to generate false trust?
11. Do ads imply more than the product research justifies?

4 Mind Watch

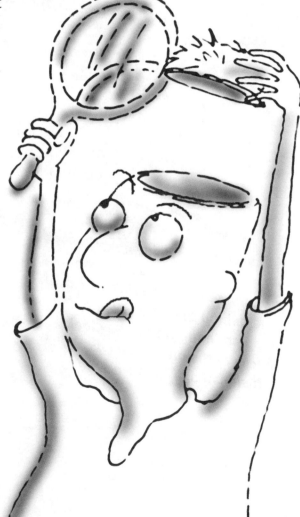

If you're going to be good at spotting bad science, you'll need to draw on the fistful of Baloney Busters and Media Alerts covered in the last two chapters. They'll help you look critically at scientific research and how it's reported and advertised in the media. But that's not enough. You'll also need to keep a mind watch, sidestepping the Mind Traps you face every day. Mind Traps are what's happening inside your head when the thinking parts of your brain shut down, function illogically, or run short of basic scientific knowledge. Then you have trouble dealing with news of scientific research.

Like other kinds of traps — even the ones that hunters use to capture lions and tigers — Mind Traps are often hidden.

Becoming aware of them is the first step to dealing with them. This chapter will help you with that. To avoid Mind Traps, you need to

STOP AND THINK, staying clear of blind-mind traps, such as simply accepting hearsay;
WATCH HOW YOU REASON, escaping logic traps, such as assuming something's true because it hasn't been disproved; and
AIM TO KNOW MORE, raising your level of scientific literacy to understand research more easily.

There are more Mind Traps than the ones listed here, but these will give you a good start recognizing mental pitfalls and avoiding them.

Folks who believe in snakelike monsters sometimes spot one swimming when river otters travel one behind the other. Rising and dipping in the water, the sleek backs of the otters can create the illusion of one long creature.

Stop and Think

It's easier to accept ideas than to question them, to ignore information than to change your views, to follow your heart instead of your head. Easier, but risky. Quacks can take advantage of people who aren't using their heads. So stop and think — it'll help you avoid these Mind Traps.

MIND TRAP 1

Grapevine Gossip

"Miracle-making moss on the Moon! Read all about it. Watch it on TV." The news must be true, or it wouldn't be reported, right? Wrong — of course. Applying Baloney Busters and Media Alerts to what you pick up from the news helps you weed out some of the bad science, poor reporting, and misleading advertising. But a lot of people don't question what they read and hear if it claims to be research. As worthless as that research might be, it often impresses and intimidates — and is mistaken for reliable information.

People who get fooled unintentionally may, in turn, lead others astray. For instance, if your friends tell you something, you're not likely to grill them about the source of their information — you just take their word for it. Even if you do ask, they likely wouldn't remember accurately. People frequently forget the source of the information they store in their memories, so if your friends' ideas have been misled by bad science, yours might be, too.

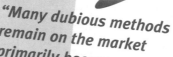

"Many dubious methods remain on the market primarily because satisfied customers offer testimonials to their worth."

— Barry Beyerstein, psychologist

ALWAYS THINK: Do I just accept hearsay, OR do I check out what I hear with reliable scientific sources?

Quacks know the strength of this informal grapevine. They encourage people to share news of a tea that appears to cure colds or a knee-rub that seems to stop stomachaches. The word spreads, and when it reaches you, you might pass it on, too.

Trust in Doubt

It's a good thing that young children are so trusting. Their lives can depend on it. "Don't touch that stove!" someone shouts, and a toddler immediately draws back her hand. A little skeptic determined to make her own discoveries would get burned.

But developing a sense of doubt should be a normal part of growing up. The same trust that can save you as a child can put you in danger as an adult. Quacks of all kinds target people who are overly trusting. They try to sell "therapies" or "medicines" to treat a lack of energy, for instance, when all that might be needed is enough sleep, exercise, and nutritious food.

MIND TRAP 2 *Fountain of Youth*

Want to be healthy, attractive, athletic, lovable, and young forever? Who doesn't? For centuries, everybody's ancestors searched for magic tonics, brews, and charms that could grant any or all of these wishes. And today, many quacks and advertisers claim they have the answers. Oh, they don't talk of magic, but they do offer false hope through their own form of potions, such as vitamin combos, pollens, special herbs, lotions, aromas, and more. Even ads for perfume imply that dabbing the right scent behind your ears can lead to romance (see Media Alert #11: Leading You On).

ALWAYS THINK: Do I simply believe what I want to, OR do I make assessments based on sound scientific information?

Seeing is believing. True — sometimes — but you might also experience a case of "believing is seeing." What you expect can affect your observations. If you take a tonic guaranteed to make you feel better, are you more or less likely to spot color in your cheeks? How might a report of a cougar in your neighborhood affect what you "see" when you spot a golden Labrador dog at dusk?

See if you can affect what your friends "see" and "hear." Gather at night in a quiet room lit only by candles, and invite everyone to tell spooky stories. Do the normal creaks and groans of a house and the movement of shadows in flickering candlelight suggest to anyone that something is lurking nearby?

Circus of Horoscopes

A little something for everybody was what famous circus owner P. T. Barnum claimed to offer. In fact, he said it was the secret of his success. It also seems to be the secret of the success of horoscope writers, who look to the skies to offer "information" about people's personalities and their futures: "You prefer a certain amount of variety in your day," reads one horoscope. "You have a need for others to like you." Yes, you — and your best friend, your grade one teacher, Uncle Harry, Ms. Crabtree at the post office, and the little kid across the street. Most horoscope statements are so general they suit almost everybody. In fact, some newspapers have accidentally mixed up the data in the horoscopes they printed without receiving any complaints of inaccuracies.

As a source of fun and games, horoscopes are fine. The problem is that many people believe them. Why? One reason seems to be what scientists call the "Barnum effect" — an unconscious tendency to read in more details than are actually contained in vague descriptions of individuals or situations. People usually recall these more detailed descriptions as if they were exactly what the horoscopes had said. Further, many people tend to remember the horoscope predictions that fit their experience, forgetting those that don't.

One newspaper staffer regularly wrote horoscope columns simply by tossing statements into a hat, pulling them out at random, and sticking them under any of the 12 birth signs, such as Aries (March 21 to April 19) and Leo (July 23 to August 22).

MIND TRAP 3

My Opinion? Ask Mary

Your friend Bob says brown eggs aren't any better for you than white eggs. But Aunt Meg claims brown eggs, like brown bread, are more nutritious. That's why she's willing to pay extra for them. If you check it out yourself, you'll discover that Bob's the one who got the facts straight: white eggs are every bit as nutritious as brown ones. The difference is simply in the color of the shell. Certain chickens lay brown eggs, and others lay white. In fact, one kind of chicken — sometimes called the Easter egg chicken — lays blue or green eggs. Now what would Aunt Meg make of those?

The point is that many so-called facts contradict one another. White eggs are less nutritious than brown eggs; white eggs are just as nutritious as brown eggs. Instead of checking out the contradictions and thinking them through, you might be tempted just to override them according to some sort of personal policy you've developed. For instance, whatever's said, you might just always choose to adopt your Aunt Meg's opinion on the subject — or the opinion of *Ragweed* magazine or Club WeKnowAll.

ALWAYS THINK: Do I handle conflicting information by lazily adopting the opinions of a favorite source, OR do I check the facts, using scientific information?

MIND TRAP 4

Forcing the Shoe That Doesn't Fit

You believe you're a terrific snowboarder — and your buddies do, too. So you were not happy to see your mother charge ahead of you on the slopes of Mount Snowsalot last Saturday. What's that, you say? You really wanted to run the slopes at a more relaxing pace? You were taking it easy while you tested a new technique? Maybe so, but aren't you just rationalizing — providing plausible but untrue reasons — to save face? Do you want to take time out to consider that your mother might be a mean snowboarder herself? No way!

Information that disagrees with assumptions you hold can make you feel uncomfortable — even downright miserable. To resolve that feeling, it's tempting to distort the information so you can bring it in line with your assumptions. That's something many folks — even scientists — do. When Dr. William Harvey (1578–1657) discovered how blood circulates through the body, he upset many doctors who assumed the body used up its blood supply, then replaced it. Instead of testing his discovery using scientific methods, they dealt with Harvey's information emotionally by concluding he was a crack-brained scientist whose theories were not worthy of their serious attention.

ALWAYS THINK: Do I reject or distort scientific information because it doesn't fit with my assumptions, OR do I try to evaluate this information objectively?

Foxy Feelings

Aesop told a tale of a hungry fox who discovered some luscious grapes hanging from a vine on a tall trellis. But no matter how high the fox leaped, he couldn't reach the grapes. After several tries, he slunk away, muttering, "I wouldn't want those grapes anyway. I see now how sour they are."

This tale led to the expression "sour grapes." It's used like this: "When Chris didn't make the baseball team, he said it was a losing team anyway — but that's just sour grapes." Chris was distorting information that disagreed with his assumptions about his pitching skills. Like the fox, he was persuading himself that what he couldn't have was no good so he was better off without it.

MIND TRAP

5 Wise Guy

"Better safe than sorry" is a bit of wisdom from the ages. Like most people, you probably rely on proverbs now and then to guide your actions and explain the workings of the world. They've been around for centuries and everybody knows them, so it's easy to assume they're true. And there's no thinking involved!

ALWAYS THINK: Do I simply trust folk wisdom, OR do I recognize that many sayings contradict one another and think things through instead?

The trouble is that proverbs often contradict one another. If you're "better safe than sorry," how do you react to advice claiming "nothing ventured, nothing gained"? If you can pick and choose proverbs to suit your needs, how useful can they really be?

What's more, folk wisdom can contradict the wisdom of science. The proverb "Lightning never strikes the same place twice" doesn't hold up under investigation. In fact, lightning bolts once struck the Empire State Building in New York City 15 times in 15 minutes.

Warring Wisdom

The world of folk wisdom is full of contradictions. Here are a few examples. Try to think of more.

Is it this way?	Or that?
• Birds of a feather flock together.	• Opposites attract.
• Look before you leap.	• He who hesitates is lost.
• You can't teach an old dog new tricks.	• It's never too late to learn.
• Fight fire with fire.	• A soft word turns away a hard blow.

MIND TRAP 6 — Cure Me — Quick!

Sheer panic can lead people to accept phony science — no matter how intelligent or knowledgeable they are. Struck by an incurable disease, for instance, many folks feel desperate to find help. They're willing to try almost anything that might cure them — even swallowing powdered rhinoceros horn. There's always a quack ready to sell a quick fix.

Other misdirected "researchers" get into the business of creating fear for fame and profit — predicting doomsdays, for instance. One was to have occurred on May 5, 2000. That's when the Moon, the Sun, and five planets — Mercury, Venus, Mars, Jupiter, and Saturn — were lined up with Earth. Without any backing from sound science, doomsdayers claimed that the combined gravitational pull of all these bodies would cause catastrophes — powerful earthquakes, supersonic winds, shifting walls of polar ice. In short, the end of the world.

May 5, 2000, came. It went. The alignment of the planets had no special effect on climate, geology, or life on Earth — but it did sell a lot of books over the years leading up to it.

> "Inspect every piece of pseudoscience and you will find a security blanket, a thumb to suck, a skirt to hold."
>
> — Isaac Asimov, science writer

ALWAYS THINK: Do I give in to fear and act without thinking, OR do I refer to sound science?

MIND TRAP 7 — Been There; Know All About It

Experiences — both bad and good — can change your feelings and opinions, often quite unconsciously. If you narrowly escaped being burned in a blazing house, you'd likely be more cautious about fire than many people are. If you won raffles frequently, you'd be less cautious about gambling. But if you don't recognize that experience can affect your views, it can mislead you and make you doubt more accurate information. You might assume, falsely, that every home contains a fire extinguisher and smoke detectors, or that the odds of winning in gambling are greater than they really are. And you might also doubt the results of home fire–prevention surveys and statistical studies of gambling if they disagree with your experience-based assumptions.

> *"The true critical thinker accepts what few people ever accept — that one cannot routinely trust perceptions and memories."*
>
> — James E. Alcock, psychologist

ALWAYS THINK: Do I let my own experiences bias the way I view new information, OR do I consider new information objectively?

MIND TRAP 8 — Making a Leap

Most people aren't the least bit comfortable with something they don't understand, so they look for a simple — often unthinking — way to interpret it. In ancient times, some people explained an eclipse by believing a sky monster had devoured the Sun or the Moon. In the 21st century, some people explain moving dots and flashes in the sky by believing in UFOs.

Occasionally, the media fuel unfounded explanations, such as these, by leaping to conclusions themselves (see Media

Alert #8: Assumption — or Fact?) — even though they have many opportunities to question people who have relevant information. For instance, if the reporters who claimed dots and flashes caught on videotapes from space missions were alien encounters had contacted NASA's Mission Control in Houston, Texas, they would have discovered a more scientific explanation. The dots are simply fast-moving spaceship debris and the flashes are falling flakes of ice.

ALWAYS THINK: Do I leap to conclusions, OR do I base my conclusions on well-founded facts?

Is an Elephant Like a Rope?

From India comes an old tale of six blind men who wanted to discover what an elephant was really like.

The first man leaned against its broad side and decided the elephant was like a wall. The next touched a tusk and concluded the elephant resembled a spear. The third man grabbed onto the trunk and declared, "The elephant is like a snake!" The fourth wrapped his arms around one thick leg and assumed the elephant was like a tree. The fifth man flapped a thin ear and said the elephant was similar to a fan. The last man simply knew the elephant was like a rope because he had felt the tail.

Jumping to conclusions made each man wrong — just as it makes most people, both male and female, wrong today.

Watch How You Reason

Your brain may be switched on and humming, but it might not always be working logically. Like everybody else, you sometimes think in circles, make wild assumptions, or get confused in other ways. Keep your brain focused to avoid these tricky Mind Traps.

MIND TRAP 9 *No Jack-of-all-trades*

Aching tooth? Talk to a dentist. When you don't have the information you need to take action, it's best to ask an expert — but only if that expert has background in an area related to your question. Unless your dentist is also a psychologist, there's no point asking for advice about Grandma's memory loss.

Yet people are often fooled by what is known as the "halo effect" — thinking experts in one field are also well informed in others — especially if they're very smart. But mathematician Dr. Countsalot of First-rate University may be no more of an expert on earthquakes than you are.

You can also be fooled into thinking that professional associations are all-purpose organizations — especially those with impressive-sounding names. For instance, the Global Association for Advancement of Research into Autotomy may be a good group to consult if you're concerned about whether your pet lizard will regrow its shed tail, but it's not likely to offer any sound information on your cat's ear infection.

One more thing: experts — individuals or associations — cannot be expected to know everything in their own fields. Information accumulates and changes quickly, making it hard to keep up to date. Besides, experts sometimes have pet theories and ideas that are not widely accepted. Even physicist and mathematician Sir Isaac Newton — one of the world's most brilliant scientists — devoted part of his life to alchemy, a blend of science and magic.

ALWAYS THINK: Do I think experts know everything, OR do I get the information I need from specialists in relevant fields?

MIND TRAP 10
Mind Trap #10: Mental Loop

Like a dog chasing its tail, human thinking can run in circles. For instance, you might say, "Tina was elected president of the student council because she has so many friends," only to argue later that Tina has so many friends because she's president of the student council. Your mind would be playing a similar loop if you fed Singaway Bird Food to your prize canary because it sings so much, then recommended Singaway to other bird owners who wanted their birds to sing. And it's just as illogical to assume that Dr. Know-It-All is an ace scientist because he's highly rated by the Super Science Association — if all you know about this association is that Dr. Know-It-All says it's excellent.

ALWAYS THINK: Do I think in circles, OR do I advance my thoughts logically, step by step?

Your Turn

What's wrong with this argument between Charlie and his sister, Laura?

Charlie: I deserve the increase I got in my allowance because my work around the house is more important than yours.

Laura: Well, my work is every bit as important.

Charlie: No, my work is clearly more important than yours because I got an increase in my allowance.

MIND TRAP 11 And Why Not?

There must be intelligent life on other planets because scientists haven't proved there isn't any, you say? Well, it's possible there's intelligent life out there, but the "proof" you offer is no proof at all. If that's all it takes to make a winning argument, you can assume a million things: Santa Claus, the tooth fairy, Superman. Just pick a fantasy and say, "You can't prove me wrong!" In fact, it's up to the person who makes a claim to back it up — not other people to disprove it.

"It's startling that people believe there are ghosts, even though science has examined ghosts for 110 years and came up with nothing but thin air."
— Paul Kurtz, philosopher

Suppose you're babysitting a five-year-old who insists there's a monster beneath the bed. You say there's no such thing and try to prove it by shining a flashlight under the bed or by laying a trail of crackers to draw the monster out. No matter what you do, the child claims the monster exists — it's invisible, it doesn't eat crackers, on and on. By this time, you're pulling your hair out. Of course, you can't expect a five-year-old to back up a claim, but you're old enough to avoid this Mind Trap yourself. Claiming that scientists — or anyone else — can't prove monsters or ghosts or little green Martians don't exist is certainly no proof that they do.

ALWAYS THINK: Do I think something's true just because it hasn't been disproved, OR do I search for proof that it is true?

MIND TRAP 12

Know a Little, Assume a Lot

No pop and chips for health-conscious Heather. She avoids food that offers mostly empty calories. In fact, everything Heather eats is chock-full of nutrients. But based on that knowledge, you can't assume her diet — as a whole — is a healthful one. Oh sure, Heather eats ample servings of bread, cereals, milk, and meat or meat substitutes every day. But what about fruits and veggies? If she's skimping on an important food group, her body isn't getting all the nutrients it needs.

What you know about part of a situation — such as what Heather eats (only foods that are healthful) — doesn't necessarily apply to the whole — her complete diet (which is not well balanced enough to be healthful despite including only healthful foods). And consider the Super Kids' Study Group: Sue's great at math, Taylor's got chemistry down pat, and Steve aces all his English tests. Even if they're working together to help one another, the group as a whole will not necessarily excel in all of those subjects: Steve may still struggle in math even with Sue's help, and Taylor, the chemistry whiz, may be hopeless at spelling.

The same applies to scientific research. A study of biking accidents among teenagers may have examined a large, random sample of these accidents, but you can't assume the research as a whole was well done. For instance, it may have gathered data only in Chicago, but applied the results to all of North America.

ALWAYS THINK: Do I think a whole study is as well done as part of it, OR do I assess the whole separately from the parts?

MIND TRAP 13 *Typically Untypical*

Teenagers, North Americans, and farmers each have typical characteristics based on statistics from scientific research — especially the mean. But that doesn't say that any particular teenager, North American, or farmer has all those characteristics. The typical student in Anywhere High School may wear jeans, slurp spaghetti, enjoy football, and hate Mozart, but you can't assume that Frankie — who attends that school — is a jeans-wearing, spaghetti-slurping, Mozart-hating football fan. In fact, he may be none of those things.

You can probably think of hundreds of other examples. A typical healthy person exercises regularly, but Cousin Henry feels great despite his decades as a couch potato. A typical hare eats only veggies, but snowshoe and arctic hares occasionally nibble meat. You get the idea. So don't assume every — or even any — individual is typical of the group.

ALWAYS THINK: Do I think that "typical" is the same as "individual," OR do I remember that the two can be very different?

By the same token, you can't dismiss research about what's typical for some group or category just because it doesn't describe a particular individual you know. The fact that your pet poodle eats bananas does not disprove research that shows the typical dog — or even the typical poodle — turns up its nose at bananas.

MIND TRAP 14 — Story Telling

Your friend Mary ate parsnips all week, and now she's zipping around town with new-found energy. Then there's Grandpa Brown. He credits parsnips with getting him up and running in the morning. Does this suggest you should race to your nearest grocer and stock up on parsnips? Hardly. Mary's burst of energy might have been the result of exercise or a host of other things that occurred that week (see Baloney Buster #18: Crowns Don't Make Kings). Further, she may have influenced Grandpa Brown's surge of pep. Tell people they'll feel better after doing something, such as eating parsnips, and they often will. That's the power of suggestion — behavior that scientists call the "placebo effect" (see Baloney Buster #10: Letting the Cat out of the Bag).

What's more, two cases — even if they're valid — don't make a reason to promote anything. Think back to what you read about sample size and its importance in applying research results to a population (see Baloney Buster #7: Size Matters). If it seems possible that parsnips generate extra energy, a few cases might interest scientists in checking out the possibility. But without a lot more evidence than the experiences of Mary and Grandpa Brown, it wouldn't make sense to assume that parsnips have any special powers. (That may be a huge relief if you happen to hate parsnips!)

ALWAYS THINK: Do I think conclusions can be based on anecdotes — stories — OR do I look for scientific evidence?

MIND TRAP 15 — All or Only

Ever heard an argument that goes like this? "Carla said that all basketball players are fast runners, but she's wrong. I have a lot of friends who are fast runners, and none of them are basketball players." There's definitely a wrinkle in that reasoning — "all" never means "only," not even close. Carla did not say that ONLY basketball players are fast runners.

At the beginning of this book, you read about graphologists who claim that creative people use circles to dot their *i*'s. To back up this conclusion, Steve Script might argue, "All the people I know who dot their *i*'s are creative." But this doesn't mean that only people who dot their *i*'s are creative. There may be lots of creative people who use tiny little dots on top of their *i*'s just like you might do. Or suppose you heard scientists report that broccoli is a good source of vitamin C. If you concluded, therefore, that broccoli is the only source of vitamin C, you'd be a victim of this Mind Trap. Other sources of vitamin C include Brussels sprouts, green bell peppers, red cabbage, strawberries, and oranges.

Advertisers often rely on their audience to think that "all" means "only" (see the Feeling Jolly example in Media Alert #11: Leading You On).

ALWAYS THINK: Do I think "all" means "only," OR do I recognize the huge difference?

MIND TRAP 16

What a Coincidence!

Plug in a lamp and the doorbell rings. E-mail your best friend at the very second he e-mails you. Coincidences like these are not as rare as you might think. In fact, they occur every day. Still, it's tempting to attach great significance to coincidences because they seem so weird. People often assume that something must have caused two events to occur together, or that one somehow caused the other (see Baloney Buster #18: Crowns Don't Make Kings). That kind of thinking is the stuff of superstitions such as, "If I put on my lucky socks, I can win my soccer game."

Think of all the times you e-mailed your best friend when he wasn't e-mailing you — and vice versa — and remember that your doorbell must have rung thousands of times without you plugging in a lamp. But then, these happenings are so ordinary and frequent that you

Your Turn

Superstition says that bad luck can strike if you walk under a ladder, spill salt, fail to forward a chain letter, spot a black cat crossing your path, and on and on. Even though there is no scientific evidence to support them, superstitions like these have been around forever. Poke fun at them by holding a party on the "unluckiest" day — Friday, the 13th. It would be especially neat if you lived on the 13th floor of an apartment building! Invite a black cat to your party, serve mis-fortune cookies, and set up a few games. To get you started, here's some of the entertainment one group of California scientists and skeptics planned for their Friday the 13th Superstition Bash:

- Limbo under the Ladder
- Salt Throwing
- Chain-letter Toss
- Mis-fortune Teller.

Add to the fun by setting up more games based on other superstitions you know.

barely notice them. If you did, it would be much easier to put the occasional coincidence into perspective.

It's no coincidence. Put 23 people in a room and there's a mathematically proven, one in two chance, that two of them will share a birthday.

People who promote supernatural claims sometimes take advantage of people who attach significance to coincidence — especially if the coincidence involves an emotional event. Let a photo of an aunt fall off your wall about the time she died and quacks may be quick to tell you that one event caused or signaled the other.

ALWAYS THINK: Do I think coincidences are significant, OR do I realize that there's usually no connection between the two events?

Rooster Reasoning

In one of Aesop's fables, a rooster reasoned: "First thing each morning, I throw back my head and start crowing. A few minutes later, the Sun rises. I must be the greatest bird in all the land because I make the Sun get up every day."
    Sad to say, this bird is not alone in his manner of thinking. People who conclude that A caused B just because A regularly came before B are practicing rooster reasoning. They're confusing cause with correlation (see Baloney Buster #18: Crowns Don't Make Kings).

MIND TRAP 17 Popular Perception

Everybody says the number of spots on a ladybug indicates its age, so it must be true. Friday's rock concert is sure to sell out because so many kids want to attend. You can't go wrong with cough syrup — everybody finds it helps cure a cough.

Each of these statements uses popularity as the reason for claiming that it's true. But popularity is relevant in only one of them — the second statement. The reasoning in the other two is faulty. The relationship between a ladybug's spots and its age is common folklore, but that doesn't make it true. Most ladybugs have all their spots within 12 hours of becoming adults. And just because many people believe in the value of cough syrup doesn't mean it actually cures their coughing. "Everybody" thinking something doesn't make it right. Nor does the fact that something is unpopular make it wrong. Watch out for this kind of faulty reasoning.

For hundreds of years, people the world over believed the Earth was flat — but that didn't make it right.

ALWAYS THINK: Do I think a statement is true just because many people do, OR do I check out the facts with scientific sources?

Your Turn

If you've ever tried the argument, "But, Dad, everybody's doing it," you've probably had a response along these lines: "Well, if everyone leapt off a bridge, would you join them?" In this case, at least, Dad is well aware that just because "everybody" is thinking or doing something doesn't necessarily make it right. But like everyone else, he probably falls into this Mind Trap now and then. Listen closely to conversations among your family and friends, and try to see when they fall into Mind Trap #17.

Aim to Know More

Being illiterate means you don't have enough reading and writing skills to do what you need to do in life. Being scientifically illiterate means you don't have the basic knowledge and understanding you need to sift the good science — and the good science reporting — from the bad.

"What we know is minute; what we are ignorant of is vast."

— Pierre Simon Laplace, mathematician, on his deathbed

It does not mean that you're lacking a huge storehouse of scientific facts, or that you're missing the skills you'd need to do science. If it did, many scientists would be scientifically illiterate in scientific disciplines outside of their own.

MIND TRAP 18 Know Better

Scientific illiteracy is a major handicap that limits people the world over. Would you believe nearly half of American adults do not know how long it takes Earth to travel around the Sun? That's what the International Center for the Advancement of Science Literacy (ICASL) discovered in recent surveys. It estimates that more than 90% of Americans are scientifically illiterate — even by standards that most people consider "soft." But don't just frown on Americans. About half the Chinese questioned by the China Association of Science and Technology didn't know that Earth revolved around the Sun once each year.

Poor science and poor science reporting can easily lead scientifically illiterate people astray. If you don't have a basic understanding of science and the scientific method, you don't know enough to ask questions. Then you tend to accept only what you're told — whether you're a judge or a juror, a politician or a voter, a retailer or a consumer, a doctor or a patient, a journalist or a reader. And that's downright dangerous.

> ALWAYS THINK: Do I accept my level of scientific literacy, OR do I keep working to increase it?

Your Turn

In his "Who's Counting" column for ABCNEWS.com in March 2000, mathematician John Allen Paulos asked: "Who Wants to Be a Sci-Savvy President?" He designed a 15-question scientific literacy quiz for the U.S. presidential candidates of the day. "All other things being equal," he wrote, "greater scientific literacy (which includes being realistic about what one doesn't know and being open to the scientific advice of others) makes for a better candidate and a better president." Here is a sample of questions from his quiz. Try them out, then check "Solutions," page 100, for the answers he gave.

- Is there any scientific evidence for the claims of astrologers?
- What strikes you as wrong about a claim that a block weighing approximately 310 pounds and having a volume of roughly 73 cubic feet has therefore a density of 4.246575342 pounds per cubic foot?
- People speak of Newtonian theory, Darwinian theory, or Einsteinian theory, and they also sometimes talk about Fred's theory, Martha's theory, or Waldo's theory about this, that, or the other thing. Is the word "theory" being used in the same way in these two sets of cases? If not, how do the two ways differ?
- What is a double-blind study? A placebo? Would you be interested in a photo opportunity with the latter at the San Diego Zoo?

◆ ◆ ◆

You're rolling now. You've been watching how your mind works as you receive news on science. You're learning to stop and think — think logically, that is, and you're making an effort to give yourself a basic scientific background. Review the summary checklist given here often, and you'll keep sidestepping those Mind Traps.

Mind Trap Checklist

STOP AND THINK

1. Do I just accept hearsay, OR do I check out what I hear with reliable scientific sources?
2. Do I simply believe what I want to, OR do I make assessments based on sound scientific information?
3. Do I handle conflicting information by lazily adopting the opinions of a favorite source, OR do I check the facts, using scientific information?
4. Do I reject or distort scientific information because it doesn't fit with my assumptions, OR do I try to evaluate this information objectively?
5. Do I simply trust folk wisdom, OR do I recognize that many sayings contradict one another and think things through instead?

6. Do I give in to fear and act without thinking, OR do I refer to sound science?
7. Do I let my own experiences bias the way I view new information, OR do I consider it objectively?
8. Do I leap to conclusions, OR do I base my conclusions on well-founded facts?

WATCH HOW YOU REASON

9. Do I think experts know everything, OR do I get the information I need from specialists in relevant fields?
10. Do I think in circles, OR do I advance my thoughts logically, step by step?
11. Do I think something's true just because it hasn't been disproved, OR do I search for proof that it is true?
12. Do I think a whole study is as well done as part of it, OR do I assess the whole separately from the parts?

13. Do I think that "typical" is the same as "individual," OR do I remember that the two can be very different?
14. Do I think conclusions can be based on anecdotes — stories — OR do I look for scientific evidence?
15. Do I think "all" means "only," OR do I recognize the huge difference?
16. Do I think coincidences are significant, OR do I realize that there's usually no connection between the two events?
17. Do I think a statement is true just because many people do, OR do I check out the facts with scientific sources?

AIM TO KNOW MORE

18. Do I accept my level of scientific literacy, OR do I keep working to increase it?

5 Winning Strategies

When you're striving to keep ahead of bad science and bad science reporting, you have to think clearly and critically and be prepared to take action. That means throwing some lifelong, winning strategies into play.

BE WARY OF "BREAKTHROUGH" SCIENCE without shutting out new ideas.

PLUG IN TO SCIENCE by exploring its basic concepts and methods, and discovering how science changes your world.

SPEAK UP FOR SCIENCE by pushing for whatever's needed to help you and others understand research better.

With strategies such as these, you're ready to roll!

Be Wary, Be Wise

Being wary, watchful, or even suspicious of scientific research is not being negative. It's using your head to protect yourself — a very positive thing to do. Ask questions, demand evidence, and insist on clarity and you empower yourself to form wiser conclusions and make better decisions.

Be Wary but Open-minded

Being wary is as essential to good science and the discovery of knowledge as it is to you. Scientists, however, promote a balance between wariness and openness to new ideas. You should, too. If you scoff at everything unfamiliar or unexplained, you risk throwing out the good with the bad. After all, there was a time when some people doubted the light bulb, and another when people failed to believe in airplanes.

"If our minds are neither too open nor too closed — we may learn more about our world and ourselves. We may even have some fun doing it."

— Joe Nickell, researcher of supernatural claims

Suspicion greeted many pioneer scientists, such as William Harvey, the medical doctor who discovered how blood circulates through the body (see Mind Trap #4: Forcing the Shoe That Doesn't Fit). When he first published his work on blood circulation, he lost the faith of many of his patients. And most scientists and medical doctors ignored his discoveries for 20 to 30 years.

Think of a wary mind as a screen window. It doesn't shut everything out, but it doesn't let it all in either. The wary person screens information through questioning.

Consider the Evidence For and Against

If you come across a totally amazing claim, some advice from an 18th-century Scottish philosopher might help you decide how much weight to give it. David Hume reasoned that support for any statement must seem more likely than whatever doesn't support the statement — if it's to be believed.

Suppose, for instance, that 5000 people at an outdoor rock concert insisted they saw the stars in the Big Dipper move apart, zoom around the Moon, then suddenly reappear in their constellation. As completely wild as this story sounds, 5000 eyewitnesses are hard to ignore. So think like Hume. It's not likely that all those people were lying or dreaming, but it's far less likely that stars would ever move like that. And if they had, millions more people would have seen them, too — but they didn't. In other words, the evidence that supports the claim is much less likely than the evidence that doesn't.

Further, the wilder the claim, the more evidence you should demand to support it — especially if it contradicts well-established science. As astronomer Carl Sagan pointed out, "Extraordinary claims demand extraordinary evidence."

"When we confuse hopes and facts, we slide into pseudoscience and superstition."

— Carl Sagan, astronomer

Draw on Baloney Busters and Media Alerts, and Sidestep

Drive a car down the road at Spook Hill, Florida, or Magnetic Hill, New Brunswick, then stop. Throw the car into neutral and it will be "drawn" back up the hill. Amazing? Not really. The reason for this weird experience has nothing to do with ghosts or magnetism. It's mostly due to an optical illusion. Look it up — there's plenty written about it — and discover the science behind what's really happening.

Many of the claims you'll come across will be far less astounding than stories of stars zooming around the Moon. You'll be able to question them, drawing on Baloney Busters and Media Alerts, and think them through, sidestepping Mind Traps. Once you get the hang of it, you can challenge the findings of any research. You'll clue in quickly when you're given too little information to form reasonable conclusions. You'll be more comfortable questioning statistics — even if you don't have a strong background in math. You'll also be more aware of some of the illogical assumptions you and others may be making. Realistically, you'll still get fooled some of the time — everybody does — but as your skills and confidence grow, you'll get better at sorting good science from bad.

Century of Super Skeptics

Asked to name outstanding skeptics of the 20th century, scholars who regularly investigate supernatural claims came up with the following, among others.

★ **Math whiz Martin Gardner,** whose books on pseudoscience — including the 1952 classic, *Fads and Fallacies in the Name of Science* — inspired skepticism in many.

★ **Astronomer Carl Sagan** — the "public's scientist" — whose books and TV shows excited the public about good science and cautioned them about bad science.

★ **Philosopher Paul Kurtz,** who founded the international Committee for the Scientific Investigation of Claims of the Paranormal (CSICOP), an organization of distinguished scholars who encourage science education and open-minded, critical research.

★ **Aerospace editor Philip J. Klass** — the "Sherlock Holmes of UFOlogy" — who has spent more than 30 years skeptically investigating claims of Unidentified Flying Objects (UFOs).

★ **Magician and escape artist Harry Houdini,** who used his knowledge of magic tricks to expose people who claimed to contact ghosts.

Plug In, Clue In

Clueing in to science isn't something you can do overnight. It's an ongoing, lifelong process — but a fun one. Start by plugging in wherever you find good science. Check for great books and magazines, quality radio and TV shows, science talks, math courses, worthy Internet sites, and so on. Above all, give yourself some direction.

Science can be "irresistibly alluring. We are talking here, after all, about us — our bodies, our world, our universe."

— Richard Flaste, science editor

Get Acquainted with Key Scientific Concepts

You might begin with a book on basic scientific literacy. *Science Matters: Achieving Scientific Literacy* by Robert Hazen and James Trefil, for example, is built on 18 broad principles that the authors think everyone should be aware of — such as "all life is connected" and "electricity and magnetism are two aspects of the same force." You might also look at James Trefil's *1001 Things Everyone Should Know about Science*.

Your Turn

If you know how a magic trick is done, you no longer believe it's magic. In his book, *Science Magic*, Martin Gardner shares several tricks that have been passed from magician to magician. Try one: Give a raw egg an energetic spin, then immediately stop it with one fingertip. Instantly lift your finger and watch. The egg will slowly spin itself. The "magic" is performed by the liquid — inside the egg — which is still swirling around.

Discover How Science Works

Become familiar with the general approach to scientific research. All fields follow the same basic pattern of investigation, so if you get "up close and personal" with one field, you'll feel more at home with the others. Read widely, visit science labs, take part in experiments at hands-on science museums, attend open houses at universities and government science departments, and talk to scientists and science educators.

Strengthen your sense of analysis by learning a bit about statistics, too. Check out plainly written — and fascinating — books such as Cooper B. Holmes's *The Honest Truth about Lying with Statistics*. You'll not only improve your understanding of statistics, but you'll realize how easily statistics can be used to mislead you.

Notice How Science Affects Society

Chemical spills in rivers, cloned organs for transplants, meteorites striking Earth. Science issues appear in the news almost every day. As someone who lives in a democracy, you have a say in how your country responds, so it's important that you understand a bit about what's going on and how it might affect you. Read widely and tune into a variety of media shows and sites. It helps to get as many facts and views as possible. Look for balanced, complete, and accurate coverage.

Danger: segasseM drawkcaB

Psst! Wanna find out what your friends and family are really saying when they're talking to you? Simply tape them as they speak, then play the tape backward. At least that's the claim made by people who believe in the notion of reverse speech. They think there are backward messages — the "voice of truth" — hidden in everybody's normal talk.

Although there is absolutely no scientific research that supports the idea of reverse speech, believers claim it's a great tool for society: it could help companies hire employees, reporters analyze politicians, and lawyers extract "evidence" from witnesses. Whoa! Think of the damage that could result from basing important decisions on something so meaningless — I mean, sselgninaem os gnihtemos.

Sharpen Your Thinking Skills

Honing your mind is not something you should work at just now and then. Make mental fitness — like physical fitness — part of your daily routine. Keep working to sift evidence from propaganda, logic from superstition, conclusions from assumptions, and science from folklore. Your powers of critical thinking need plenty of exercise, but the workouts can be fun as well as useful. Pick up some books or software programs that offer brain bafflers, mind teasers, and logic puzzles. Enjoy.

"Science is not about memorizing stuffy words and useless facts. Science is about asking questions — the 'dumber' and simpler the better — and impishly, persistently trying to get sensible answers."

— Marc Abrahams, editor and creator of the Ig Nobel Prize Ceremony

Speak Up, Speak Out

If you're wary of bad science and you're plugging in to good science, you're already making great strides to improve your skills in assessing research. But there's another strategy that can help you. It calls for speaking up and speaking out — to scientists, the media, educators, and the government. Join other voices who are calling for more complete, easy-to-understand scientific information and better funding for quality science education and research. Here are four ways

Million-dollar Challenge

It's one thing to challenge someone and another to "put your money where your mouth is." But that's just what James Randi of the James Randi Educational Foundation has done. He and his organization support and conduct research into supernatural claims. As a professional magician and escape artist, he is well suited to spot any tricks.

For decades, Randi offered $10 000 for "the performance of any paranormal, occult, or supernatural event, under proper observing conditions." Hundreds tried to claim it, including a high school principal who said his touch could mummify food and a librarian/scientist who tried to use a brass tube and a wire to find ancient ruins on a map. But no claim has ever been proven.

More recently, Randi's Foundation set up the even more impressive $1 000 000 Paranormal Challenge. The money is reserved to "reward and publicize any legitimate demonstration of paranormal ability under proper test conditions." Don't hold your breath waiting for someone to earn it.

you can do this: spur the scientists, move the media, encourage the educators, and guide the government.

Spur the Scientists

Scientists want to be understood and supported by the media and the public — people like you. But they don't always realize it's part of their job to explain what they're doing, how and why. Show them you want to know. Invite scientists to talk to classes, clubs, and other groups. Encourage them to share their research methods and findings in terms everybody — including the media — can understand.

Move the Media

If you want more science reporting, call for it. Let your newspaper, TV, and radio producers know. Some scientific research never gets passed on to the public because media managers think it's not entertaining or not visual enough — or because their sponsors wouldn't like the study results.

"The news and entertainment media that give so much play to unscience do not give equal time to science."

— Dyan Machan, journalist

And while you're talking to the media, tell them you want to get both good news and bad. Too often science reporters focus on scary stories about the possible danger in some procedures or products. But when these same things later prove harmless, it's considered "non-news" and goes unreported or, at least, underreported.

Your Turn

- If your local newspaper publishes horoscopes, ask the editor to label them "for entertainment only," and not to print them on the personal advice pages.
- If you write a letter to a newspaper or magazine editor to complain about bad science reporting and it gets published, you have a chance to win a Citizen Sane Award for your efforts. Send your published entry to CSICOP, P.O. Box 703, Amherst, NY 14226. The staff of CSICOP (Committee for the Scientific Investigation of Claims of the Paranormal) vote for a winner each year.

Encourage complete, clear, accurate, and responsible reporting on science. Insist on getting the details you need to feel confident about the research. And ask reporters to name other research studies on the same subject.

In general, become a media watchdog. Call or write to criticize any promotion of false science, and point out the harm it can generate. Even when it's presented in fun by talk show hosts, phony science gets a lot of attention it doesn't deserve.

Encourage the Educators

Public schools, colleges, and universities belong to you. So you have the right to insist they provide a strong science education — including courses in the ways that science affects society. You also have the right to demand training in critical thinking and logic at all grade levels. Support teachers and community leaders who lobby for better science programs and resources.

Your Turn

- Find out how your public and school libraries support science education. Do they have strong selections of recent science books? If not, suggest that they do. Ask your friends and family to make the same suggestion.
- Ask community centers and night school programs that offer fortune-telling courses, such as teacup reading, to advertise them as "for recreation only."

Guide the Government

Take your demands for science education to the government and ask for support and funds. Other requests you could make? Encourage richer funding for research so scientists don't have to depend as much on dollars from companies and associations that might influence the results. And ask for support for agencies that work to protect consumers from advertising that misrepresents scientific research.

◆ ◆ ◆

"Science lets us view the world with new eyes, exploring backward in time, looking through space, and discovering unity in the workings of the cosmos."

— Robert Hazen and James Trefil, scientists

Cures for more diseases that kill people, robots that carry out trillions of instructions per second, and discoveries so amazing they're not even dreamed of. During this century, scientific research will change the world you live in. In fact, you probably can't even imagine what your life will be like just 50 years from today. No one can.

That's a call for you to be ready — to be better informed about science than people have ever had to be before. As scientific research mushrooms, so do the number of weak and phony studies, claims, and media reports — and your risk of being fooled rockets. So be wary, plug in, speak up. Refer to the checklist included here, and take action. It's up to you to make a difference!

Winning Strategies Checklist

BE WARY, BE WISE

- Be wary of "breakthrough" science without shutting out new ideas.
- Consider if the evidence that supports a claim seems more or less likely than the evidence that doesn't support it.
- Think through claims by drawing on Baloney Busters and Media Alerts, and sidestepping Mind Traps.

PLUG IN, CLUE IN

- Get acquainted with key scientific concepts.
- Discover how science works.
- Notice how science affects society.
- Sharpen your thinking skills.

SPEAK UP, SPEAK OUT

- Spur the scientists to explain what they're doing, how, and why.
- Move the media to provide more solid science reporting.
- Encourage the educators to offer a strong education in science, logic, and critical thinking.
- Guide the government to fund scientific research and education, and consumer protection agencies.

WHERE TO GET HELP

Magazines

ODYSSEY: Adventures in Science
Published 9 times per year
30 Grove Street, Ste. C, Peterborough, NH, USA 03458
(603) 924-7209

Science World
Published 14 times per year
P.O. Box 3710, Jefferson City, MO, USA 65102-9957
1-800-724-6527 (in USA), 1-800-268-3848 (in Canada)

Skeptical Inquirer: The Magazine for Science and Reason
(for advanced readers)
Published 6 times per year
Box 703, Amherst, NY, USA 14226-0703
1-800-634-1610 (in USA), (716) 636-1425 (in Canada)

YES Mag: Canada's Science Magazine for Kids
Published 6 times per year
3968 Long Gun Place, Victoria, BC, Canada V8N 3A9
info@yesmag.bc.ca

Simons, Lewis M., "Archaeoraptor Fossil Trail," in
National Geographic, October 2000, pp. 128–32.
(an example of science and science-reporting gone wrong)

Internet Sites

Addresses of Internet sites can change often. If you
have trouble finding a site, check with a librarian for
current listings.

Committee for the Scientific Investigation of Claims of
   the Paranormal (CSICOP)
http://www.csicop.org
Young Skeptics
http://www.csicop.org/youngskeptics
Skeptical Museum of the Paranormal
http://www.csicop.org/skeptiseum

Internet Sites (cont.)

James Randi Educational Foundation
http://www.randi.org

Quackwatch
http://www.quackwatch.com

Quirks & Quarks
http://www.radio.cbc.ca/programs/quirks

Skeptic's Dictionary
http://www.skepdic.com

Books

Flaste, Richard, ed. *The New York Times Book of Science Literacy: What Everyone Needs to Know from Newton to the Knuckleball.* Toronto: Random House of Canada, 1991.

Gardner, Martin. *aha! Gotcha: Paradoxes to Puzzle and Delight.* New York: W.H. Freeman, 1982.

Gardner, Martin. *Science Magic.* New York: Sterling, 1997.

Hazen, Robert, and Trefil, James. *Science Matters: Achieving Scientific Literacy.* New York: Doubleday, 1991.

Holmes, Cooper B. *The Honest Truth About Lying with Statistics.* Springfield, IL: Charles C Thomas, 1990.

Ingram, Jay. *The Science of Everyday Life.* Markham: Viking Press, 1989.

Klein, David, and Klein, Marymae E. *How Do You Know It's True?* New York: Charles Scribner's Sons, 1984.

Paulos, John Allen. *A Mathematician Reads the Newspaper.* New York: Basic Books, 1995.

Randi, James. *An Encyclopedia of Claims, Frauds, and Hoaxes of the Occult and Supernatural.* New York: St. Martin's Press, 1995.

Sagan, Carl. *The Demon-Haunted World: Science as a Candle in the Dark.* New York: Random House, 1995.

Books (cont.)

Trefil, James. *1001 Things Everyone Should Know about Science.* New York: Doubleday, 1992.

Wade, Nicholas; Dean, Cornelia; and Dieke, William A., eds. *The New York Times Book of Science Literacy, Volume 11: The Environment from Your Backyard to the Ocean Floor.* Toronto: Random House of Canada, 1994.

Wolke, Robert L. *What Einstein Didn't Know: Scientific Answers to Everyday Questions.* New York: Dell, 1997.

Wolke, Robert L. *What Einstein Told His Barber: More Scientific Answers to Everyday Questions.* New York: Dell, 2000.

Glossary

Arithmetical average: The mean — the sum of a set of figures divided by the number of figures in the set.

Average: A mean, median, or mode. In everyday language, "average" is often used in place of "mean."

Biased sample: A sample — part of the whole, or population, being studied — that does not truly represent the population.

Barnum effect: A tendency to read in more details than are actually contained in vague descriptions of individuals or situations.

Cause: A relationship between two things when one brings about the other.

Control group: People or things with characteristics similar to those in the test group of an experiment.

Correlation: A relationship between two things that vary together. One may increase as the other increases; one may decrease as the other decreases; or an increase in one may be related to a decrease in the other. Correlation does NOT mean cause.

Data-dredging: Focusing on data that support a theory while ignoring data that don't.

Doomsday: A day of tremendous calamity; often meaning the end of the world.

Double-blind technique: A method of avoiding bias during research experiments. Neither the experimenters nor the test subjects know exactly who or what is receiving which treatment.

Halo effect: A generalization from the quality of one trait to other traits belonging to the same person or group.

Jargon: Technical words used by a special group, profession, or occupation.

Mean: The sum of a set of figures divided by the number of figures in the set.

Median: The middle value in a set of figures. Half the figures are worth the same or less than the median figure.

Mode: The figure that appears most often in a set of figures.

Percentile: The figure at which a given percentage of the values in a set fall at or below that figure. The 50th percentile is the same as the median.

Placebo: An action or thing that has no real effect, even though subjects in an experiment may believe that it has.

Population: The entire group being studied. Usually there are too many things or individuals in a population to study each one separately.

Pseudoscience: A false science. Methods or theories that wrongly presume to have a basis in science.

Random sample: A sample — part of the whole, or population, being studied — in which each individual or thing had an equal chance of being selected.

Sample: Part of the whole, or population. A sufficient number of people or things to provide reliable information about the population.

Scientifically illiterate: Lacking a basic knowledge and understanding of science and the scientific method.

Statistics. Mathematics used to collect, organize, calculate, and describe data.

Statistically significant: A study result that likely did not happen by chance alone.

Theory: In science, a logical idea or explanation supported by a body of scientific knowledge.

Solutions

Your Turn, page 25

(d). See Baloney Buster #17: False Illusion for a discussion about the precision with which these scientists decided to report their results!

Your Turn, page 35

Your median grade would be 80%. If you had taken only English, French, Biology, and Math, your median grade would be 76%.

Your Turn, page 36

Beth's allowance falls into the 30th percentile.

Your Turn, page 41

If you wanted your parents to let you toss 8 cabbages instead of 6, you could say, "Bugs attacked 4 of the cabbages, and a fungus attacked 4 of the cabbages." That's true, but of course, you'd be hoping that your parents wouldn't discover that some of the cabbages that had been attacked by bugs had ALSO been attacked by a fungus.

Your Turn, page 48

How about this sentence? "Fences corral cattle."

Your Turn, page 52

Before you agreed with the reporter's conclusions, you'd at least need to compare the number of deaths per number of airplane passengers over the years. You'd also need to compare distances flown.

Your Turn, page 56

(d).

Your Turn, page 81

Here are the answers Paulos provided for part of his "Who Wants to Be a Sci-Savvy President?" science literacy quiz for the U.S. presidential candidates of the year 2000. If you answered something roughly similar, give yourself a huge pat on the back — then run for elected office in your country.

- No.
- The answer is more precise than possible given the approximate nature of the weight and volume.
- A scientific theory is an interconnected and coherent collection of statements supported directly by evidence and indirectly by the statements' relation to each other and to other accepted bodies of evidence. Another quite distinct meaning for the term is an unproved assumption or a personal belief.
- An experimental design in which neither the experimenters nor the subjects know who is receiving the new treatment and who is receiving the placebo. The latter is sometimes an inert substance, such as a sugar pill, generally a substance or procedure that has no physical effect. No.INDEX

Index